Oriole Cullen

V&A Publishing

First published by V&A Publishing, 2009
V&A Publishing
Victoria and Albert Museum
South Kensington
London SW7 2RL

Distributed in North America
by Harry N. Abrams, Inc., New York

Hardback edition
ISBN 978 1 85177 557 6
Library of Congress Control Number 2008937533

10 9 8 7 6 5 4 3 2 1
2013 2012 2011 2010 2009

A catalogue record for this book is available
from the British Library.

Illustrations: Lawrence Mynott
Designer: Co Studio Design
Copy-editor: Miranda Harrison
New V&A photography by Richard Davis,
V&A Photographic Studio

Front jacket illustration: Lawrence Mynott, 2008
Back jacket illustration: Christian Dior *Haute Couture*,
Paris, autumn/winter 2007
Endpaper sketches by Robyn Neald (Special Edition only)

Printed in Italy by Graphicom

V&A Publishing
Victoria and Albert Museum
South Kensington
London SW7 2RL
www.vam.ac.uk

Contents

Foreword   *John Galliano* 7

Introduction   *Oriole Cullen* 9

A Personal View   *Stephen Jones* 13

Inspiration 26
Cecil Beaton and the V&A 48

Creation 50
The Hatbox 74

The Salon 76
The Turban 92

The Client 94

Milliners' Biographies 118

Notes 123

Further Reading 124

Museum Collections 124

Acknowledgements 126

Picture Credits 127

Index 128

Foreword
John Galliano

Stephen Jones and John Galliano put the finishing touches on a model for Christian Dior's *Haute Couture*, autumn/winter 2008.

It's very hard to write a foreword for someone who you work with and admire. It's even harder when you are asked to write about a subject that is *their* field of expertise and merely your fascination – so, instead, I will tell you why I wear hats and why I love them... and why I am so lucky to have Stephen Jones as my friend and collaborator all these years.

You shouldn't ask 'why do you wear a hat?' What you really should be asking is 'why are you not?' I can't imagine leaving the house without a hat. How can a look be complete without a hat? From a cap to a full-on fascinator, the hat is the accent, the exclamation mark, the finishing note that punctuates the whole look. I apply this to myself as much as to the collections I work on. Where do you think 'thinking caps' got their name from?!

Hats change and enhance – indeed they complete a silhouette. Always work up as well as down. You are meant to dress top to toe, so don't forget the final flourish. A face is so much more photogenic when framed with a crown, a boater, a brim, an air of mystique... To imagine a look without a hat is like imagining an English teapot with no lid, or takeaway coffees without their tops. It just won't do.

Men and women *should* wear hats and enjoy them. Don't just keep them for best – make an effort every day! You don't walk about with bare feet, so why should you be bareheaded? One moment they can turn heads, the next they can disguise and protect you from curious eyes. They are as much your alibi for that bad hair day or late night as the *only* date to take to Ascot, the Races, the society wedding. Think of the city gent or Charlie Chaplin without a bowler; Robin Hood without his cap; rappers or rock stars minus their baseball caps; even the Queen without her crown – the image just doesn't work. There is a hat style for all seasons, all faces, all moments. Hats are barometers of our time, of class, of style, and they have the power to condense function and frivolity into one.

I am thrilled that Stephen Jones has not only gathered this exhibition of treasures together, but has asked me to write a foreword to this 'Anthology of Love'. I remember the first time we met – it was in a club, in the eighties, and I was a student at St Martin's School of Art who was obsessed with his work. The first time I asked him if he would do some hats for me he just turned, looked at me, and said, 'I don't think so, dear!' I am so glad he had a change of heart! Just as I wouldn't leave the house without a hat, I couldn't do a show without Stephen Jones. He conjures up creations that bring Galliano and Dior shows to life. He is the frosting to any collection he touches. Just as every mood and occasion and every room in my house has a different hat, Stephen Jones – like my hat addiction – is someone I cannot do without. I raise my hat to him! Enjoy!

Les Grandes Modes de Paris
N.º 116   Pl. 1272

Supplement

Chapeau Eliane

19, Rue des Petits-Champs

Robe d'après midi

exécutée par Paul Poiret

Introduction
Oriole Cullen

Opposite page: Fashion illustration from the magazine *Les Grandes Modes de Paris-Revue de l'Elegance*, August 1910.

Right: The close-fitting cloche of the 1920s was practical yet eminently stylish, 1927

Hats: An Anthology by Stephen Jones is a collaboration between the Victoria and Albert Museum and one of the fashion world's foremost milliners, Stephen Jones. The V&A's significant hat collection is a revealing and exciting record of the changes in headgear over the past 17 centuries. While the hats in the collection are usually displayed as part of an ensemble or within an accessories display, both this book and the exhibition of the same title open up the archive in much greater depth. Taking the expert viewpoint of a milliner, *Hats: An Anthology by Stephen Jones* uncovers the rich seam of fashion, style, inspiration, craft and technique inherent in every hat.

Over the past hundred years a number of international cities could lay claim to being the creative centre of the millinery world. Paris in the early twentieth century was the heart of production for the vast frothy hats considered the ultimate fashion adornment, and also for the later contrasting streamlined cloche hats of the 1920s. American millinery led the way in the 1930s and '40s, with key designers in New York, Chicago and Los Angeles producing hats that encompassed the whimsical style of that era. The post-war New Look and the subsequent space-age creations emanated from Paris, but by the 1980s the focus had turned to London where it has since remained.

Today hats are often worn for practical matters, such as keeping warm or for formal occasions such as weddings. With these opposite ends of the scale typically representing hats, it is easy to forget that between the casual woolly cap and formal broad-brimmed straw there is a world of headgear and a myriad of styles, shapes and sizes that can be worn for any and every possible occasion. Contrary to what might be assumed, the wearing of a hat is an accessible and non-exclusive practice open to those in all walks of life. Stylish hat-wearers are not just bespoke millinery clients – many hat trends have come directly from street fashion. In 1938, English author Ethyle Campbell recalled a visit to New York where she marvelled at the availability of stylish, mass-produced and inexpensive clothing, including a 'most attractive little black suede hat' for the price of just 50 cents. 'What a Godsend for the woman of slender means who has to keep up appearances!'[1] Nearly fifty years later, a 1985 survey of hat wearers recorded the opinions of fashion student Philippa Esling, who wore a tassled fur hat made from an old scarf belonging to her mother and a gold curtain tie-back found in her old flat (p.11, left). She felt that 'Stephen Jones and Bernstock Speirs have really brought hats back into the limelight, but as few people are able to spend eighty pounds on a designer hat the obvious answer is DIY'.[2]

As the National Collection of Art and Design, the V&A has always sought to inspire and inform its visitors, and to this end has retained close links with the creative industries. A long-time visitor and supporter of the Museum, Stephen Jones has frequented the V&A since his earliest days as a student in London. A key inspiration behind this anthology was the collaborative work that took place over 30 years ago between the Museum and another creative – fashion photographer and illustrator Cecil Beaton. With the V&A's seminal exhibition of 1971, *Fashion: An Anthology by Cecil Beaton* (below), Beaton helped to put fashion firmly on the museum agenda. Concerned with what he saw as the disappearing world of *haute couture* he approached the V&A to propose an extensive exhibition and subsequent donation of *haute-couture* clothing, collected from both fashion designers and their clients. While Beaton's

Below: Exhibition shot from the V&A's *Fashion: An Anthology by Cecil Beaton*, 1971. The focus on fashion and the dramatic set design afforded an entirely new experience to the museum visitor.

Above: Student Philippa Esling wears a home-made hat, *Etc. Magazine*, 1985.

Above middle: Stephen Jones in the North Court store at the V&A, 2007.

Above right: Women stitching felt hats in a British hat factory, *c.*1900.

approach in the 1970s was to form a new and important fashion archive, Stephen Jones's approach was to investigate and explore (and be inspired by) what was already held within the Museum's archives – similarly highlighting hats as an important social and historical item of dress.

The structure of this book and exhibition came from the hats themselves. Stephen Jones and I began our investigation on 2 April 2007. In the V&A's North Court store for fashion and textiles, we set up our 'studio' – a small table with a card backdrop and a mannequin head – and opened the cupboard doors. With an open brief and no set agenda, Jones chose hats from the shelves purely on the basis of what attracted him, passing them back to be photographed as his thoughts on each piece were recorded. We would spend the next year going through cupboards, stores and other museum collections, looking at what amounted to thousands of hats. As the hats emerged, key themes became apparent, such as the natural world, historicism, exoticism and modernism.

While hats have been worn for thousands of years, millinery is a comparatively recent area. Established over the past three hundred years, millinery concentrates on a more decorative and light-hearted approach to hat-wearing, as opposed to protective, religious and status matters often conferred by hats. The hat industry, which thrived in this country from the seventeenth century until the 1950s, was primarily concerned with the large-scale production of standard menswear styles and shapes. However Stephen Jones is a model milliner, primarily concerned with creating beautiful, often intricate, handmade hats for women. As such this book and exhibition focus on the hat from the millinery point of view, with the majority of pieces consisting of women's hats from the twentieth century – a rich period for millinery. Men's hats are included where they are particularly significant or have had a key influence on millinery design.

By combining Jones's responses to the V&A hats collection with curatorial observations in a broader context, *Hats: An Anthology by Stephen Jones* is an entertaining exploration of the hat as a universal symbol, worn throughout time by different cultures, societies and religions. This anthology aims to demonstrate the importance of the hat as an accessory that has the power instantly to impart a message of authority, affiliation, individuality, propriety, rebellion and – not least – style.

A Personal View
Stephen Jones

Opposite page: Marlene Dietrich
wearing a signature beret in the
film *Witness for the Prosecution*, 1957.

Right: Gertrude Shilling, Ascot,
1973. Known as the 'Ascot Mascot',
Shilling delighted the crowds at
the Ascot races for over 30 years
with her spectacular hats. Here she
is wearing a hat that celebrated
Britain's joining of the European
Economic Community in 1973.

Far right: Stephen Jones, black
knitted hat, autumn/winter 2005.
A simple black hat gives a timeless
modern look.

Hats are *the* important accessory. In fact, when worn with verve, they are often the *raison d'être* of many an outfit. But when magazines write articles on accessories, often they myopically feature only bags and shoes. Now I have nothing against Miucca or Manolo, Louis or Lulu, but what about gloves, scarves, jewels – and hats? Why are they remaindered to the Timbuktu of fashion when they are in fact its Shangri-La? Where would Tutankhamen be without his headdress, or Anna Piaggi without her veil? Or for that matter Chanel without the boater or Stüssy without the baseball cap?

A hat makes clothing identifiable, dramatic – and, most importantly, Fashion. There are so many expressions marking the importance of a hat. It's the cherry on the cake, the dot on the 'i', the exclamation mark; the fashion focus. Everyone from showgirls to dictators knows that by wearing a hat they will be the centre of attention. It need not be as striking as one of millinery maven Gertrude Shilling's extravaganzas, who grabbed the headlines in the 1970s in her pro-Europe headgear (above). It can be as low-key as the restrained chic of film star Marlene Dietrich's beret basque (see p.12). Does this mean hats are only for those who want to be the centre of attention? Not at all, but they confer a sense of presence and poise to the wearer that, in my mind, cannot be achieved through clothing or other accessories.

Fashion designers know this very well when they use hats to punctuate fashion shows. I remember listening to a radio programme many years ago in which Malcolm McLaren, founder of punk, reminded the interviewer that the vocabulary of fashion is frighteningly small. In a fashion show, hats dramatically expand that vocabulary, giving accent to particular outfits

and defining the look of the season. I am lucky enough to have collaborated for many years with John Galliano, and recently questioned him as to why he attached so much importance to hats and why they feature so strongly in his shows both at Galliano and Dior. He looked surprised, and asked why his interest should stop at the neckline as it was above there that things really got interesting. Every season he finds an innovative creative harmony between hair, make-up, jewellery and hats.

More everyday hats like that beret of Dietrich's or an anonymous baseball cap allow the wearer to blend into daily life, whilst the detailing tells a more intimate story of personal style and taste; the feel of velvet, a blazing red satin lining, a fabulous embroidery. Of course, hats can simply be about protection – be they compulsory sun-hats for school children in Australia, or fur bonnets in the Arctic Circle – but the wearers always customize the hats with their own personality. Although I try to give the hats in my own collection as much spirit and character as possible, they are ultimately inanimate objects and only come into being when worn. Initially I will place them on top of the head of a client and experiment, trying to find the correct angle, but after a while they become an extension of the person themselves, not simply something that is worn like clothing.

This is the magical power of a hat – its ability to reflect the character of individuals but also to transform them into someone else. This eloquent transformation can be from woman to lady, from geek to heartthrob, from romantic to dominatrix and so on. Strangely, when this magic is put into a hat it can look light-hearted and convincing, but if put into clothes they become costume. The magic is elusive, but maybe it's because adorning your head is such a primary act of being. In Papua New Guinea, for instance, the tribesmen may go almost naked but they always wear more feathers in their hair than burlesque performer Dita Von Teese (see p.100). A baby looks cutest with a little bow in its top-knot; when I put a veil on a bride-to-be she invariably bursts into tears; and a crown is the most potent symbol of royalty. Maybe it's because we communicate with our heads that anything that changes them in shape, colour or decoration is a striking statement. Not for nothing was Colin McDowell's 1997 book on hats entitled *Hats: Status, Style and Glamour*. In part the magic is composed of the visual clues that the hat contains. Does it look futuristic or vintage? Parisian or Polynesian? Happy or sad? Sculptural or dumpy? Creative or familiar?

These are the tools that milliners use in making a hat. Of course the materials are felt and straw, flowers and feathers, but when clients are buying a hat they are buying a dream, not reality. A favourite anecdote of mine is about Mr John, New York's pre-eminent milliner (see p.15). In the 1960s he created a turban for a client, and when he handed her the bill for $100 she told him the price was outrageous. He then unravelled the turban and said, 'Madam, the materials are free'.

Above left: Stephen Jones for John Galliano, 'Fish Bone' hat, autumn/ winter 1999.

Above right: A man of the Wahgi tribe, of the highlands of Papua New Guinea, wears a feathered headdress.

In English the word 'milliner' comes from the word 'Milan', which was known for its high-quality trimmings and accessories, but it is in the French word *modiste* that hats find their true expression. In the eighteenth century, at the time of Rose Bertin (Marie Antoinette's favourite milliner and fashion creator), dresses were made by *couturières* while *modistes* made all the trimmings and consequently the hats. Women's hats were born as being little trifles; whimsical frivolities in lace, ribbon and straw. The much sterner materials of felt, gilt embroidery and ostrich feathers were mainly reserved for male headwear, and were used by tailors and hatters.

Milliner Mr John, fitting a hat to a client's head, 1962.

Milliners themselves are strange beings. Rose Bertin (1747-1813) was a true fashion diva, arrogant and impetuous, and since that time milliners have tended to have a determined sense of self and a certain flamboyant eccentricity. Of course many milliners veer off path and become dress designers (such as Lucile, Lanvin, Chanel, Fath, Halston, Adolfo, Mr John – even the first sketches that Dior sold were to Claude St Cyr, the milliner). But milliners usually see themselves as people not in the mainstream of fashion but up some fantastical tributary, made from glamour and veiling.

Liverpool

For almost 30 years now hats have been my life, but I was definitely a late starter in the fashion world. Unlike many other designers or fashion creators I was not whipping up a ballgown for Mummy aged three. Life for me started on the Wirral peninsula in Cheshire, plonked between the Dee and Mersey estuaries with the hills of Snowdonia to the left and the bright lights of early sixties Liverpool to my right. At prep and then public school in Liverpool I was always better in art than other subjects, although I was very much an all-rounder. I could not say that I had a flair for art, as that implies a self-awareness that I really didn't possess and that my school certainly didn't teach. (They specialized at rugby and running the Empire.)

The highlight of my school year was Founder's Day at the Gothic Anglican Cathedral, where I marvelled at the vastness of the still unfinished building (below left). The largest cathedral in Britain, it was started in 1904 and finished in 1978. Luckily my great-great-grandfather, who had a haulage company called Robert Jones, got the contract for hauling the red sandstone (below right). I also made my own trips to the dramatic modernist Roman Catholic Cathedral, known locally as 'Paddy's Wigwam'. Built in five years from concrete, from 1962 to 1967, its amazing space-age design in the round with mirrored baroque torchères has had a huge influence on me. During the holidays my mother wheeled me round the Walker Art Gallery in Liverpool – part of the series of unbelievably pompous buildings in the centre of the city – and we had outings to the Tudor half-timbered Speke Hall. Aged seven I was an expert at the Hogarth line, and knew every National Trust property in the North West. However, as a teenager I really wanted to get up to London, as Liverpool seemed bleak and permanently on strike.

Opposite page, left: Charles James, satin jacket, 1937.

Opposite page, right: The dramatic Art Deco lines of the auditorium at the Liverpool Philharmonic Hall. Following a fire the Hall was redesigned by architect Herbert Rowse, and re-opened to the public in 1939.

Below left: The Liverpool skyline, detailing the two famous cathedrals – a lasting source of inspiration for Stephen Jones.

Below right: Excavation of Liverpool's Anglican Cathedral, showing a Robert Jones haulage truck.

London

It was in the summer of 1975, as an art foundation student at High Wycombe College of Art, that I first visited the V&A – to see the exhibition *Fashion from 1900–1939*. This was a revelatory experience. Most extraordinary for me was the fabulous sculptural padded Charles James jacket of 1937 (above left), which reminded me of the undulating interior of Liverpool's Art Deco Philharmonic Hall (above right). For the first time I had an inkling that I would like to be part of the fashion world. I applied and amazingly was accepted at St Martin's School of Art (now Central Saint Martins) to do women's fashion. I knew I was the token male. Sadly, in the first year my work did not progress as everyone hoped. My classmates were whipping up those ballgowns whilst I was struggling to thread a needle. My efforts at tailoring were particularly dreadful, but I loved the classes as they were instructed by Mr Peter Lewis Crown, the designer-owner of the London couture house, Lachasse. He regaled us with gossip about Princess Margaret whilst we attempted to pad-stitch collars so they 'rolled like a cream horn' (trying to coax a 3-D shape from unwilling 2-D fabric). To improve my technique I was accepted on a summer placement as a temporary worker in his tailoring workroom (the words 'intern', 'work experience' or '*stagière*' had not yet been invented).

The world of tailoring did not seem like the white heat of technology to a 19-year-old punk, but next door to the tailoring workroom was the millinery workroom. Hats for me were an unknown quantity, but most important were the two ladies making them. Mrs Hex and her assistant Lily were a couple of larger-than-life characters, who laughed as hard as they worked. This seemed like the place to be. I asked Mr Crown for a transfer from tailoring to millinery, and he called Mrs Hex to the office. She enquired if I had ever made a hat, and then stated that she could not accept me until she had seen a hat that I had made from start to finish. That weekend I worked flat-out and constructed a pillbox hat out of turquoise crêpe de Chine with silver piping, mounted on card. This was trimmed with a blue plastic iris, sprayed silver, that my mother had got free with petrol in the mid 1960s. I didn't know that flowers for hats were made from silk – when I showed my efforts to Mrs Hex on the Monday morning she okayed the hat, and said the plastic flower was 'very modern'. I transferred to millinery and after the first day was hooked, knowing that this was what I wanted to do in life. What seemed wonderful to me at the time was that hats were a solid constructed object that seemed to create maximum effect for minimum effort. Little did I realize that hats are almost more complex and time-consuming to make than clothes.

1978: Hats in the modern world

I worked at Lachasse during the holidays, learning millinery techniques from the ever-patient Mrs Hex, but I really didn't know anything about the millinery universe. Sure I had worn a cap to school and a boater in the summer, but in 1978 fashion terms, hats were irrelevant. In 1976 Johny Rotten may have worn a beret (above right), but in my topsy-turvy aesthetic, a big straw trimmed with daisies seemed not archaic but a strangely anarchic counterpoint to the familiar punk iconography of safety pins, rubber and black lipstick. To me hats came from a bizarre world of haughty arched eyebrows and weird formalized rituals.

Because of hats I became interested in the history of fashion, in particular the mannered world of Horst, Balenciaga and Barbara Goalen (above left), which I gleaned from a few dusty copies of old *Vogues* in the college library. I loved the extravagant postures and the glamorous silhouettes, which were far removed from my tutors' tastes in happy clappy Kenzo or beige Calvin Klein. They hated it.

1979: Out into the unknown

Museum studies were an important part of the college curriculum, every Monday my classmates and I visiting the Museum of Childhood, Natural History Museum or Imperial War Museum. At the V&A we were not encouraged to visit the Costume Court, as learning about the history of fashion was considered incidental. Our time was spent in the glass, ceramic, metalwork and plaster cast rooms – and most importantly the tearoom. The St Martin's fashion system of historical research, idea development and final drawing had not been introduced (this was to start with John Galliano), so trying to find out about the greats of British design, whether Cecil Beaton, Norman Hartnell or Robin Day, was well nigh impossible. Consequently these seemed all the more fascinating, and my final collection at St Martin's in 1979 (see p.19) featured dysfunctional white satin presentation dresses for debutantes complete with broken Perspex tiaras and dead seagulls representing the obligatory Prince of Wales feathers.

The creative atmosphere when I left college was in flux. The huge changes wrought by punk in 1976 had lost their energy, and the vacuum that was created by its demise was filled first by the New Wave and secondly the New Romantics. They used historical inspiration to create something original and 'Now', which seemed to be in tune with my way of thinking. London's notorious Blitz club, started by Steve Strange in 1979, was a magnet for these movements and

their aficionados, and I was a regular. Here was where my hats were first seen on my friends Kim Bowen (p.19, right), Chessie von Thyssen and Princess Julia, as well as Boy George and Spandau Ballet. Through Steve, in the September of 1980, I opened my first millinery salon in the basement of the ultra stylish boutique 'PX' in Endell Street, Covent Garden. To my complete surprise, within a year of leaving college I was in business (below right).

The V&A

Around this time I bought a second-hand copy of the slim catalogue of an exhibition held at the V&A in 1971 – *Fashion: An Anthology by Cecil Beaton* (top right). The rarefied world that Beaton described in his foreword was that of his high-society friends of the 1940s, '50s and '60s, who had donated favourite designer outfits to be shown in the exhibition and which still form the core of the V&A's twentieth-century costume collection. The catalogue described forgotten names like Dessès, Norell and Cavanagh, as well as the greats like Dior, Balenciaga and St Laurent. Since then I have met many of the people who contributed to this exhibition – the designer Michael Haynes; Andrew Logan who made mannequins for the Schiaparelli section; Verne Lambert who was the fashion advisor for the exhibition; Madeleine Ginsburg who wrote the original catalogue and who has contributed invaluable information to the current exhibition, and lastly Lawrence Mynott, who was shown around the exhibition personally by Cecil and has drawn the magical illustrations for this book. The exhibition was hugely influential in putting contemporary fashion within a museum. Beaton's international reputation and showmanship ensured its success, and foreshadowed the hugely successful costume exhibitions curated by Diana Vreeland after she joined the Metropolitan Museum in New York in 1972.

In 1982, when the Costume Court at the V&A was being refurbished, I had a call from the senior costume and textiles curator Valerie Mendes. A special millinery cabinet was being created. The hat collection at the V&A was legendary, from examples of Balenciaga's finest collected by Beaton through to the most extravagant eighteenth-century poke bonnets that could grace a Yohji Yamamoto fashion show of today (see p.21). I was amazed and honoured when she asked if the V&A could purchase a Stephen Jones hat. I had only been going for two years, but had started to make my mark with hats for a bizarrely polarized range of clients from Boy George (below) to the Princess of Wales. Having a hat in the V&A really was the cherry on the cake, and I thought that now I could comfortably retire (aged 25!). The hat that I made used an origami-type technique of folding, unlike the traditional technique of blocking, which resulted in a rhythmic sculptural shape. The silhouette however was directly inspired by the hats of the Queen Mother in her 1939 portraits at Buckingham Palace by Cecil Beaton, and in fact the coral satin on the under-brim came from the closing-down sale of Edward Rayne who had been her shoemaker.

FASHION: AN ANTHOLOGY BY CECIL BEATON

Above: Invitation to *Fashion: An Anthology by Cecil Beaton*, V&A, 1971. The graphic lines echo those of the publicity shot from the Beaton-designed film *My Fair Lady*, 1964; Stephen Jones business card, featuring 'Gerlinde' hat from his first collection, autumn/winter 1980.

Left: Singer Boy George in a Stephen Jones hat, 1980s.

Opposite page: Yohji Yamamoto, giant wedding hat, 1998.

Since then, one of my greatest treats has been going to see the V&A hat collection to be reminded of the extravagances of yesteryear and the assurance and flair of millinery maestros of the past. I have always had my favourites – Jacques Fath's astonishing asymmetric hats from the 1950s, created by his milliner Svend, are a combination of Parisian erotique and Cadillac pizzazz; an English Rococo *bergère* hat of exquisite hand-plaited straw, trimmed with fragile blue ribbon like a Gainsborough painting; and more recently Philip Treacy's whirlwind of luminous fuchsia goose feathers (below left).

I had been talking to the V&A for many years about a possible collaboration, and gradually started to formulate an idea for an exhibition. Our idea was to delve into the V&A archives of over 2000 hats with co-curator Oriole Cullen, and to create new hats based on this research. That idea evolved considerably, and although the V&A archive forms the nucleus of the display, the exhibition is also peppered with additions from other British collections including Bath, Stockport, Luton, the Museum of London and the Royal Collection. There are also contributions from institutions in Los Angeles, New York, Paris, Vienna, Berlin and from private collectors around the world. In addition, the V&A archive has been brought up-to-date with contributions from young guns of the millinery world such as Noel Stewart and Sawa Nakazawa etc. Finally there are Stephen Jones hats from my own collection and from my collaborations with other fashion designers, including Comme des Garçons (below right), Giles, Marc Jacobs and Christian Dior.

A milliner in the archives

I started my research in the V&A on 2 April 2007. I approached the day with trepidation, as I really tried to come to this project without preconceptions. One of the disadvantages of being in the world of hats for so long is that one falls into the trap of pigeonholing designs into particular types. I did not want to see everything with the eye of a British 49-year-old white male milliner. Alternatively, I didn't want to be anyone else but simply to remain neutral. However, in trying to be this Biblical Solomon I realized that I was denying the emotion that is the cornerstone of great millinery. I always think that to be a good milliner you have to be a good listener, and when I relaxed and listened to the hats they spoke volumes.

Looking through my own archive was also a roller coaster down memory lane. Much had been organized by my assistant Lesley Robeson for my 25 year retrospective exhibitions at Dover Street Market in 2005, hosted by Rei Kawakubo in London and Tokyo, but what was strange was comparing my own hats to the V&A archive. How different was my rendition of

Far left: Philip Treacy, pink goose feather hat, 1995. This hat was worn by singer Kylie Minogue on the cover of *Tatler* magazine, July 1995. V&A: T.182–1996.

Left: Stephen Jones for Comme des Garçons, crown, spring/summer 2006. Photographed backstage at the Comme des Garçons show, Paris.

Stephen Jones, 'Wash and Go' hat, 1999. The acrylic form simulates water splashing around the head.

a 1940s hat from the real thing; how delicate an authentic paste tiara looked in comparison with the chandelier-sized construction that I had made! How did my little top-knot of 2001 square to that by Vladzio d'Attainville, Balenciaga's milliner? The results of this research are in my collections for spring/summer and autumn/winter 2009.

Visits to other institutions were equally rewarding. Curators were delighted that I was looking at their millinery collections, so often overlooked by researchers wanting to cherry-pick iconic Vionnet or Dior outfits, never a funny charming beige felt or a 1910 toque resplendent with two dead pheasants. Sometimes I honed in on curators' favourite hats, but often I and Oriole (or Adèle, my assistant in America) were left to poke around dark cupboards ourselves in an incredible adventure into the past. Finding Dame Margot Fonteyn's Dior arrow cloche of 1947 in Bath was unbelievable (see p.24), as I had just used it as inspiration for a hat in Dior's 60th anniversary Versailles show. An Anubis mask of 2500BC in Harrogate was mentioned by a friend, and Audrey Hepburn's Beaton-designed straw cloche from *My Fair Lady* I found squished in the bottom of a box in Warner Bros corporate archive in Hollywood, after a lead

Opposite page: Stephen Jones for Christian Dior *Haute Couture*, 'Arrow' hat, autumn/winter 2007. Inspired by an original Dior design from 1949.

Below: The original Dior 'Arrow' hat, sketched by illustrator René Bouché in 1949.

Right: Coptic fez hat made from woven metallic fabric, 1100–1499. V&A: T.45–1899; (top right) Stephen Jones, ballet shoes hat, Soho Collection, autumn/winter 1982. Jones found inspiration for this hat while walking down London's St Martin's Lane, where he saw miniature ballet shoes in the window of dance shop Freed of London. V&A: T.62– 1983; (bottom left) Philip Treacy, pampas grass rasta hat for Rifat Ozbek, 1991. V&A: T.933– 1994; (bottom right) Caroline Reboux, fur and silk ribbon hat, 1865–70. Purported to have belonged to Empress Eugénie of France. V&A: T.375–1974.

from designer L'Wren Scott. Less famous hats were equally as notable – a Tudor knitted beret at the V&A that John Galliano would die for, or a 2-inch miniature stetson as a 1940s Christmas tree decoration in the private collection of Wendy Anne Rosen in Los Angeles.

The criteria for choosing hats for the exhibition were surprisingly straightforward – a delicious brim line, spectacular detailing, an intriguing provenance (p.25, bottom right), the 'Cecil Factor', and even designs that somehow linked past, present and future (p.25, top left). Some of the most captivating hats were included on a whim, just as I create one of my own collections.

This is my very personal anthology of hats, a mish-mash of dates, places, stories and illusion that are squished into a sense of order by a mad hatter's logic. It is by no means a learned encyclopaedia, nor an accurate chronology; I will leave that to other more erudite authors. It is my own viewpoint of where hats come from, how they are made, where they are sold and the extraordinary people who wear them.

Chapeau!
Stephen Jones

Inspiration is the beginning of the life cycle of a hat. As milliners are inspired, so they must pass this frisson of excitement onto the hat and the client. Hats have to be a mirror of their age with a touch of whimsy. Historically, a knight's helmet was trimmed with a feather, which was a gift from their wives or girlfriends. A jewel made a simple Tudor beret more individual, Victorian floral bonnets might feature a caterpillar munching a nasturtium. In modern times, hats should inspire the client by embracing the novelty of the unexpected – as fashion doyenne Anna Piaggi says, hats are the ultimate frivolity.

What inspires the milliner? Ideas can come from anywhere. The list is endless. Photographs, paintings, daily life, etiquette, old movies, fish & chips. Music, the internet, travel, your boy/girlfriend, an enemy. A good mood, a bad day, pebbles. France, the future, perfume, strangers.

For my part, I simply live my life and put it into a hat. To that extent, my hats are autobiographical. Of course I have my favourite inspirations, such as film, history, travel and most importantly architecture, where style and fashion are made permanent. I always think it strange when people ask me if my ideas ever dry up. For me that has never been an issue – having too many ideas and trying to edit is the problem!

Stephen Jones

Designers have often turned to museum collections for inspiration. Stephen Jones recalls his time as a fashion student at St Martin's School of Art (now Central Saint Martins) in the 1970s, when he and his classmates were encouraged to go to museums to study and draw objects to inspire their design:

It was more than the actual objects, it was the whole world of museums… whether they had a funny little dusty ticket [on the objects] or whether they had been redone and made very modern – it was that whole atmosphere that was interesting… We rarely if ever drew the costumes, we were encouraged to focus on items as diverse as porcelain and glass and to incorporate these ideas into new forms of fashion design.[1]

It may be this diverse training which lies behind Jones's thinking that 'anything can be a hat'. He will take a piece of paper, artfully scrunch it up and place it on the side of the head to illustrate his point. Indeed the idea that 'anything' can be a hat is evident in the work of many of the great milliners. Jones himself has made hats from materials as unusual and surprising as Perspex, lollipop sticks and burnt matches. Alongside hats made from newspaper and from coconut fibres, Schiaparelli was famously inspired to create a 'shoe hat' (above), fashioning a heeled stiletto from felt, while in the 1990s Kirsten Woodward created a hat for Chanel that consisted of a miniature armchair placed on top of the head.

Unencumbered by prescribed matters of garment construction such as sleeves, neck openings and waistlines, the hat can remain very true to its original source of inspiration. It can impart to the onlooker an instant and immediate recognition of the wit and whimsy of its point of inception. Inspiration from nature has always been close to the heart of the milliner, with flowers, straw and feathers being key elements of the milliner's trade, yet some of the most outrageous and witty hat designs have been inspired by advances in technology or equally by mundane and everyday items

Above: House sketch for Schiaparelli's hat designs based on shoes, 1937.

Opposite page: Stephen Jones for John Galliano, 'Thunderbird' hat, 1996. Made from wooden lollipop sticks.

Opposite page: Stephen Jones, Kon-tiki hat made from bulrushes, spring/summer 1993.

Above: Milliner Madame Agnès creating hats from lacquered wood shavings. Shortages of materials during the Second World War only served to increase the creativity of many well-known milliners.

Right: Philip Treacy, David Beckham hat, 2003. Treacy proves that inspiration can come from a myriad of sources.

In a 1914 *New York Times* report on the collections in Paris, there was a special mention for the inventiveness of the fashionable milliner Suzanne Talbot's designs and her treatment of ribbons, wings and flowers: 'She gave them a bath of glycerine and then put them between two heavy rollers, until the surface was very much like Japanese lacquer'.[2] This kind of experimentation and constant inspiration gained from new materials and methods is key to the successful milliner's art.

In the early 1940s, wartime restrictions acted as a catalyst for a number of high-profile milliners. In New York, the milliner Lilly Daché used Lucite, an acrylic glass, in place of ribbon and kitchen twine as a substitute for straw.[3] Bes-Ben, 'Chicago's mad-hatter', created exquisite hats from everyday household items, such as a Dutch bonnet made from a tea towel and edged with napkin rings.[4] Rationing and shortages in London drove Aage Thaarup to source his materials from junk shops: 'What incredible finds I made. An overmantel with a lovely yellow fringe; cleaned up, the fringe was good for half a dozen hats'.[5] In Paris, meanwhile, milliner Madame Agnès used lacquered wood shavings from interior designer, Jean Dunand. These examples serve to reinforce Stephen Jones's point that the inspiration for a hat can come from anywhere and has done for many centuries.

Left: Stephen Jones stands in front of a rock formation in Utah, 2007 which would inspire his 'Bryce' hat.

Opposite page: Stephen Jones, 'Bryce' hat, spring/summer 2008.

A trip to Utah inspired Stephen Jones's spring/summer 2008 collection 'Desert Rose', featuring hats inspired by rock formations, open skies and desert blooms. Desert Rose had followed a number of collections inspired by Jones's travels.

At the time that we began work on this anthology, Jones had decided to turn to home for inspiration and was in the process of designing a collection inspired by London's Covent Garden, the home of Stephen Jones Millinery. He looked at all aspects of the area, from the historic fruit, vegetable and flower market to the Royal Opera House and the London Transport Museum (see pp.34-5) and to one of the most famous filmsets in Covent Garden, that of *My Fair Lady* (featuring the artful costumes of Cecil Beaton). During a research visit that we made to Hatworks Museum in Stockport, Jones was finishing the sketches of these hats. As the train moved out of London, Jones drew his signature head – comprising a simple vertical line, an oval face and a fluttering eyelid elegantly suggested by a small curled line (see p.34). Above each head, a hat began to form – a flat cap decorated with miniature vegetables inspired by the stall holders of the old fruit and vegetable market (see p.35); a ballerina's feathered headdress, influenced by the dancers of the Royal Opera House; a leather trilby representing a London taxi, lined with a print of the A-Z and a small 'for hire' sign on the hat band. The hats ranged from a ribbed knit 'workman's cap', finished with a black glaze as though covered in tar, to a beautiful top hat decorated with a rose in colours inspired by the pink tie, white shirt and grey suit of Professor Higgins in *My Fair Lady*. The diverse types of hat, the various techniques used and the assortment of references demonstrate the extent of Jones's own points of inspiration.

Selection of ephemera which inspires Stephen Jones's design process and the resulting hats: (above) 'Folly' hat, (below) 'RHS' hat, both spring/summer 2005; (opposite top) 'Tube hat', (opposite below) 'Costermonger' hat, both Covent Garden Collection, autumn/winter 2008.

Underground beret felt
red white blue,
multi lines in the back mounted
on I.Tube.

-KEEPS LONDON GOING

Costermonger

From Wikipedia, the free encyclopedia

A **costermonger** was a street seller of fruit and vegetables, derived from the words *costard* (a type of apple) and *monger*, i.e. "seller", came to be particularly associated with the "barrow boys" of London who would sell their produce from a wheelbarrow or wheeled market stall.

Costermongers have existed in London since at least the 16th century, when they were mentioned by Shakespeare. They probably were most numerous during the Victorian era, when there were said to be over 30,000 in 1860. They gained a fairly unsavoury reputation for their "low habits, general improvidence, love of gambling, total want of education, disregard for lawful marriage ceremonies, and their use of a peculiar slang language" (John Camden Hotten, *The Slang Dictionary*, 1859). Costermongers were notoriously competitive; respected "elder statespeople" in the costermonger community were elected as pearly kings and queens to keep the peace between rival costermongers.

However, crimes such as theft were actually rare among costermongers themselves, especially in an open market where they tended to look out for one another. Even common thieves preferred to prey on shop owners rather than costermongers, who were inclined to dispense "*street justice*".

The activities and lifestyles of 19th century costermongers are comprehensively documented in *London Labour and the London Poor*, a four volume collection of very erudite and well-researched articles by Henry Mayhew.

The antihero star of *Look Back in Anger* (1956) by playwright John Osborne is a costermonger who

On our first day of assessing the V&A hat collection for this anthology, the first hat to be chosen was a hat by the world-famous couturier Balenciaga (below). A golden straw cap decorated with a mass of straw leaves and berries, it was designed to be worn directly on top of the head. Thrust into a cupboard, with little time to get his bearings, Jones breathed a sigh of relief on examining the label on this our 'first hat'. 'Thank God it is a Balenciaga!' was his response to this significant choice.

As our research progressed, several key themes emerged. The natural world was an obvious source of inspiration for many of the hats. Straw, flowers and feathers (and often full birds) are perennial favourites of millinery; while other natural themes such as the elements, animals and plants also provided points of inspiration. Sea-life was represented in technicolour by London milliner Simone Mirman's 1960s hat, 'La Langoustine Fantasia' (p.37) – a bright coral, yellow and turquoise headband with a mass of fabric tentacles curling down to the shoulders. This would inspire Jones to create his 'Sea Anenome' hat for his spring/summer 2009 collection.

Below: Balenciaga, straw beret decorated with straw leaves and berries, c.1950. Gift of Miss Catherine Hunt. V&A: T.115–1970.

Opposite page: Simone Mirman, 'Langoustine Fantasia' hat, 1960s. V&A: T.186–1983.

Below: Burlesque performer
Immodesty Blaize wearing a
Stephen Jones 'Carnival' tricorne
from his autumn/winter collection
of 2005.

Opposite right: Pink and green
organza turban by Madame
Paulette, 1960, V&A: T46-1977.

Opposite bottom right: Stephen
Jones on the catwalk holding hats
he designed for Jean-Paul Gaultier,
Paris, 1984.

Not surprisingly for a museum collection, the theme of historicism was very evident. Historic pieces, the styles of which were clearly a source point for many subsequent hats, included a Coptic fez dating from 1100–1400AD. This popular shape still endures today (and was worn by the young Stephen Jones in the Culture Club video for *'Do You Really Want to Hurt Me'*). The silhouette of an eighteenth-century black satin tricorn was clearly echoed in a 1930s Caroline Reboux feather tricorn, and was later reflected in a lavender velvet Stephen Jones tricorn worn by the Burlesque artist Immodesty Blaize (p.38). The top hat, a source of inspiration for many whimsical and miniature modern versions, was represented in all its glory by Prince Albert's black top hat. A 1970s leather Malyard hood, with a tightly fitting cap and a scalloped edged leather veil, referenced medieval headwear. This cap was in turn interpreted by Jones in a PVC version for his own autumn/winter 2009 collection (see p.41).

Exoticism was another key theme. The lure of the East, with its turbans and oriental fabrics, seems to provide a constant trove of millinery ideas to be reinterpreted. The styles in the Museum collection range from a fashionable early nineteenth-century silk turban to a 1930s Caroline Reboux bird-of-paradise hat, and a 1960s green-and-fuchsia chiffon turban with pompom by Madame Paulette (above left).

Opposite page: George Malyard, leather cloche hat with scalloped leather veil, 1968. V&A: T.346–1985.

Above: Stephen Jones sketch, PVC cloche and veil, autumn/winter 2009. This hat was inspired by the Malyard leather hood in the V&A archive.

Right: Caroline Reboux, silk and bird of paradise feather hat, c.1935. Worn and given by Sybil, Marchioness of Cholmondeley. V&A: T.375–1974

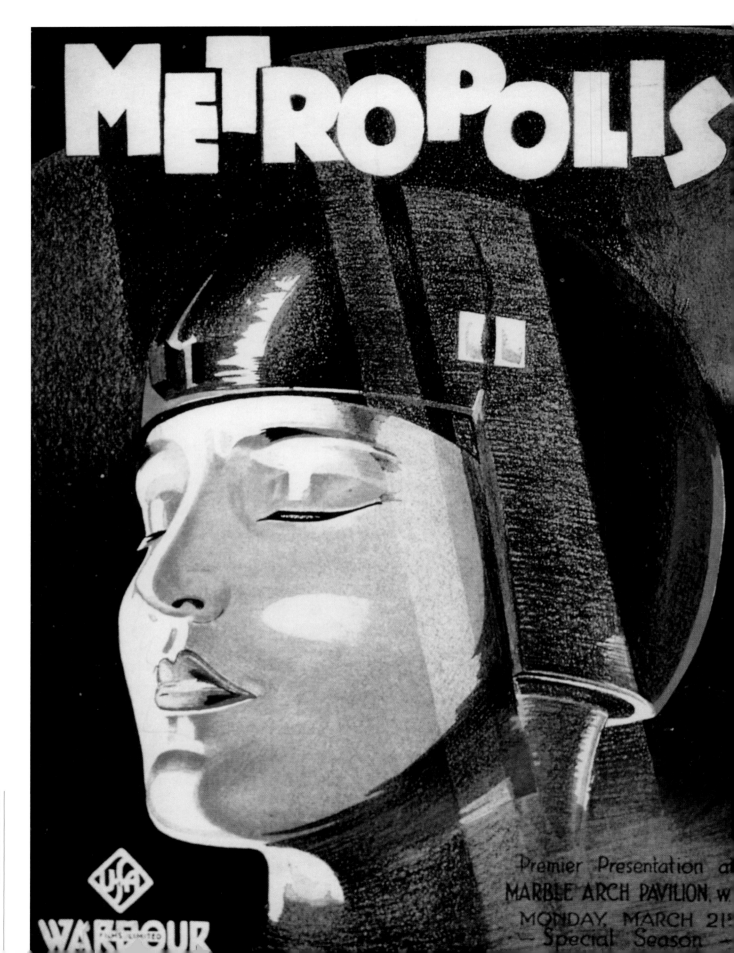

Opposite page: Poster advertising
director Fritz Lang's seminal
science fiction film, *Metropolis*,
1927, which crystallised aspects of
modernity in design.

Below: A key source of inspiration
for Stephen Jones is the 1939
film, *The Women*. Starring
Norma Shearer, Joan Crawford
and Rosalind Russell and Joan
Fontaine, it featured costumes and
dramatic hats designed by Adrian.

Many milliners have also been inspired
by the Modern Age, with architecture,
speed, travel and film (p.42), as important
points of reference. Milliner Graham
Smith's black velvet Pirelli skull cap of
1985 supports a mask-like face veil, edged
with miniature velvet tyre treads, while the
'Coniston' hat by Frederick Fox, former
milliner to the Queen, evokes speed with
its sculptured folds flaring out to one side
(see p.44). (Coniston Water in Britain's Lake
District was the site of Donald Campbell's
successful attempt to break the world
water speed record in 1955.) Michael of
Lachasse's 'Martian's Claw' of 1955 clasps
the head with curling talons that encircle
the forehead, recalling the popular science
fiction of the time (p.45).

Above: Frederick Fox, 'Coniston', 2000. Made of black velvet with bird of paradise feathers. Gift of Sir Frederick Fox. V&A: T.33–2003.

Left: Graham Smith, black velvet Pirelli skull cap, 1985. Designed for the 1985 Pirelli calendar, the hat's veil is edged with the pattern of the P6 Pirelli tyre treadmarks in velvet appliqué. V&A: T.480–1985.

Opposite page: Michael of Lachasse, 'Martian's claw' wedding headdress, 1955. Gift of Mrs June Gordon Gottschalk (worn on her wedding day). V&A: T.398–1988.

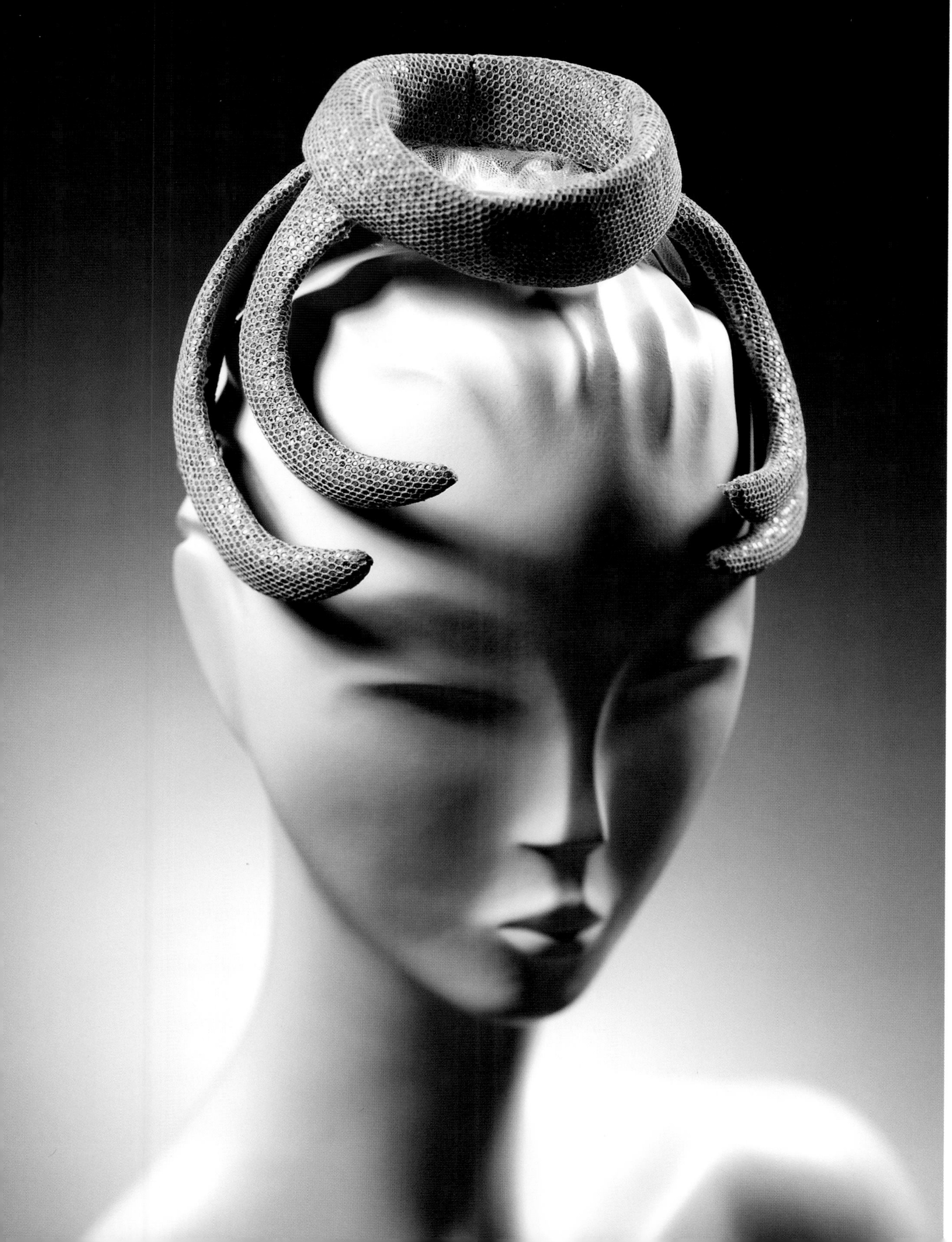

Opposite page: Stephen Jones for Galliano, 'Orchid' hat, spring/summer 2008.

Above (left and right): Stephen Jones, 'Still Life' hat depicting a rose and painter's brush. Working drawings for 'Still Life' hat.

Presented with the challenge of combining such a miscellany of hats into a cohesive whole, the word 'anthology' is particularly appropriate. The origin of the word 'anthology' lies in the Greek *anthos*, a flower, and *logia*, to collect – a gathering of flowers. As Cecil Beaton noted in his introduction to his 1971 V&A catalogue: 'I comforted myself that an anthology, by its very nature, is always incomplete'.[6] Faced by the thousands of hats we had looked at and the task of reducing this to a displayable number, Beaton's words offered reassurance. The selection of hats was indeed comparable to a metaphoric gathering of flowers, a random assembly of beautiful and eye-catching pieces, picked on a whim to be displayed in an exhibition evoking a fantastical classical garden.

CECIL BEATON
AND THE V&A

Many of the stunning and captivating hats featured in *Hats: An Anthology by Stephen Jones* came to the V&A thanks to Cecil Beaton's foresight and flair in extracting the finest examples of clothing and headwear from some of the world's most stylish women.

For over 50 years, photographer, illustrator and theatre designer Cecil Beaton was closely involved, both personally and professionally, in the world of fashion. His interest in fashion began with dressing up his sisters in fantasy costumes as subjects for his early experiments in photographic portraiture. While at Cambridge he indulged his interest through membership of the Amateur Dramatic Company and the Marlowe Players. In 1925 he left Cambridge without graduating, and gradually established a career by taking portraits of London's young social set. Having been engaged as fashion photographer and illustrator by Condé Nast's *Vogue*, he went on to be an official war photographer during the Second World War. After the war he began designing sets and costumes for film and theatre.

In 1954 Beaton wrote *The Glass of Fashion*, a personal view of the fashion world from the beginning of the twentieth century. Alongside the actual clothes and fashions, he focused on individuals and innovators. His close personal links to many of these people would later become an important factor in his decision to form a collection of the best examples of twentieth-century *haute couture*.

Above: Cecil Beaton photographed in front of the costume for the lead dancer in the Ascot scene of the film *My Fair Lady*.

Right: Cecil Beaton paints
the finishing touches on a hat
designed for the 1946 Broadway
stage production of Lady
Windermere's Fan.

Below: Audrey Hepburn dressed
in a costume designed by Cecil
Beaton for the Ascot scene of the
film *My Fair Lady*, 1964.

In 1969 Beaton contacted the V&A to propose an exhibition of the finest examples of dress and fashion – resulting in the pioneering display *Fashion: An Anthology by Cecil Beaton* in 1971. He brought his experience as a set-designer and art director to the overall presentation, working with designer Michael Haynes to create an exhibition which included a Surrealist section, a miniature Dior *haute couture* salon, double-height display windows, revolving mannequins, lighting effects and dynamic graphics. This gave the museum audience a completely new environment in which to experience clothing on display. Beaton loved and wore hats; they played a small but significant role in his anthology of 1971. The inclusion of the hats in the catalogue demonstrated the important role that they played in terms of dress over the course of the twentieth century. The show highlighted key examples of head gear from the Beaton collection which was subsequently donated to the Museum.

Over 35 years on from Beaton's exhibition, his energetic, eclectic yet informative approach has inspired Stephen Jones to pay tribute by taking a similar stance – a combination of creative designer and connoisseur – to the world of hats. The link is particularly apt as Beaton not only included several of his own hats in his donation to the Museum but he was also responsible for some of the most famous hats depicted in film. He designed the hats worn in the Ascot scene of *My Fair Lady*, starring Audrey Hepburn, and was awarded two Oscars for the film's costume design and art direction. One of the original black-and-white oversized hats (each had their own unique and dramatic silhouette), was generously lent by the Warner Brothers archive to appear in the exhibition *Hats: An Anthology by Stephen Jones*.

Creation.

The Bias, egg irons, wire. Stiffener, buckram, blocks. Feathers and flowers. Felt and straw. Furs. Silks. Ribbon… The millinery workroom is a strange and unusual place. Half Aladdin's cave and half artist's studio, hats are coaxed into life with 90% perspiration and 10% inspiration. Steaming and stretching heavy fabrics into three dimensions involves hours of work. As ballet dancers must make pirouettes look totally natural when their feet are in agony, a milliner must torture straw into doing what it doesn't want to do and make the results look effortless and spontaneous. Hats start their lives as sketches, then become dimensional prototypes pinned onto the most important thing in the millinery workroom – a *poupée*. This calico-covered head, which is our equivalent of a tailor's dummy, enables us to construct *toiles* from which we can work out the shape and trimming of a hat. From this form, we make a block or mould for the fabrics to a particular shape, or simply use it as a guide for something more free form. Many of the construction techniques have not changed in a hundred years, but today endangered bird-of-paradise plumes are replaced with dyed chicken feathers, ciré ribbons with plastics, and we use aerosol glue not rabbit-skin glue! For me the most important thing within the creative process is keeping the essence of the original concept alive, whilst allowing the hat to develop in its own way. I often think hats make themselves. I just nudge them along!

Stephen Jones

Left: Dior workroom, Paris.

Below: The salon at Stephen Jones Millinery, Covent Garden, 2008.

Opposite page: Milliner Mitsumi Kinoshita applying flowers to a veiled hat at Stephen Jones Millinery, Covent Garden, 2008.

Model millinery works on a similar system to *haute couture*, where every aspect of a garment is intricately crafted by hand. The time, skill and materials used to create a *haute-couture* gown is reflected in the significant prices of such garments with only a very small group of customers able to afford a couture wardrobe. Model hats are similarly crafted, but – due to their size, and the lack of necessity for fastenings, internal undergarments and numerous fittings on each part of the body – they are comparatively much more accessible to the customer. The milliner's salon and workroom are busy throughout the year.

The public side of the model millinery house is the shop, often referred to as the salon, with studio, workroom and offices usually based on the same site. At Stephen Jones in Covent Garden, large interior screens in the shop separate the sales area from the showroom behind, where meetings with private clients take place. From this space, doors lead off to offices on the same floor and to the all-important workroom on the floor below.

Inside the model millinery workroom

Most model millinery houses retain a workroom of specialist milliners who physically create and put together their collections. Milliners with different skills are required for the multitude of shapes and effects that are created each season. Some will be specialists in working with fine fabrics, some at creating three-dimensional shapes, others at working with straw or fur and some focusing particularly on trimmings. The model milliners' success lies in the skill and talent of the team that they create to support them.

Lesley Robeson has worked as Stephen Jones's main assistant for the past twenty years. Her position allows her to 'see the whole picture', from working on the research with Jones, to liaising with clients and to developing hats with the Stephen Jones millinery team. Accordingly 'working with Stephen Jones there is never a dull moment and you're constantly learning. Stephen will have an original idea and if he starts early on a collection he will change his mind four times, but saying that, the last hat you make for a collection is always the best'.[1] Robeson's highly energetic, no-nonsense Glaswegian approach acts as a perfect foil to Jones' charm. As we speak at Stephen Jones Millinery, Covent Garden, Robeson is laying out images of V&A exhibition hats; organising Jones's trip to the Dior workrooms in Paris the following morning; and overseeing Marc Jacobs' cruise collection hats being finished off by the millinery workroom and due in New York the following day. She is also directing numerous phonecalls – Katie Grand, über fashion editor, to speak to Stephen; Belgian designer Walter van Bierendonck with a query regarding their collaboration; an important Japanese client with a picture request. Meanwhile Stephen's cousin from New Zealand has arrived, and the fashion writer Camilla Morton pops by to say hello. 'Working with Stephen is never boring', says Robeson.

Opposite page: John Galliano, autumn/winter, 2002. Model wearing a blanket hat finished by Stephen Jones, minutes before appearing on the catwalk.

Right: Stephen Jones prepares the blanket hat backstage at John Galliano's autumn/winter 2002 show.

The Stephen Jones workroom is based beneath the shop in Covent Garden. As Jones says, 'a millinery workroom is always in an attic or a basement'.[2] The space is divided into two sections, split by a staircase. The back section is the 'soft workroom' where soft unstructured hats are made and where model hats are blocked – the process that gives shape to a structured hat. The block is a wooden form carved especially to the milliner's order for a particular hat. Today Britain's remaining specialist block makers are mostly located in the historic centre of Luton. A felt or straw hood is fitted, steamed and teased into shape over this block. The front section of the workroom is the 'model millinery workroom'. Here each and every hat created is made entirely by hand, from start to finish (see p.57). (The Stephen Jones diffusion line hats for Jonesboy and Miss Jones are sometimes assembled by outworkers, but always come back to the Covent Garden workrooms to be overseen and handfinished.)

Craig West has been head of the soft workroom for the past 14 years. He enjoys the unpredictability and challenges of working with Stephen Jones and his various clients: 'One day the brief might be "medieval knights from outer space", and you have to take up the challenge and create something'. For West it's not just about creating 'one-off' hats, but something that can be put into production and will also be a commercial success. He is dedicated to the difficult job of keeping the character and personality of each collection in every piece that is designed for the diffusion lines, Jonesboy and Miss Jones. The soft workroom operates using a mixture of clothing techniques alongside millinery skills, often using shoe and bag materials (which are a good weight for hats). Fabrics are frequently dyed on-site to obtain a particular colour and finish, and paint effects are another method used to decorate particular pieces. West observes, 'You have to be ready for everything, as you never know whether you'll be making hats out of neoprene one week and struggling to sew pieces of plywood together the next'.[3]

Above: Shelves of ribbons and trimmings at Stephen Jones Millinery, Covent Garden, 2008.

Below left: Woven hat labels, c.1915. Machine embroidered onto silk, these labels would be cut to fit inside the crown of the hat.

Right: Deborah Miller, head of the model millinery workroom at Stephen Jones Millinery, Covent Garden, 2008.

Below: Milliner Véronique Tissières works at the large cutting table in the trimmings workroom, Stephen Jones Millinery, Covent Garden, 2008.

The head of the model millinery workroom is Deborah Miller (above), who has been at Stephen Jones since 1983, shortly after he opened his first shop. As a young milliner, who had previously worked at the prestigious workrooms of milliners Dolores and Frederick Fox, Miller was interviewed in Stephen Jones's first premises in a garret in London's Wardour Street. The space had a sloping floor, and she was given a high chair with wheels on which to sit. She recalls spending most of the interview trying to stop herself from sliding across the room.[4]

From 1983 to 1988 Stephen Jones was based at Lexington Street with the workroom and showrooms divided by a screen. The staff consisted of Stephen's assistant, a trimmer, Deborah Miller and a Dutch student, Bouke. At the time Jones was very much involved with the making of the hats. In 1988 the business moved to Heddon Street, where it was based for seven years, until moving to its current premises in Great Queen Street in 1995. For this last move Jones and Miller worked out the design of the workroom space using a scale model of the shop with miniature paper furniture.[5]

Left: Headpieces assembled on a temporary line strung across the workroom. The volume taken up by the finished hats requires every bit of space to be used for storage. Stephen Jones Millinery, Covent Garden, 2008.

Below: Milliners at work around a long table in the model millinery workroom, Stephen Jones Millinery, Covent Garden, 2008

Opposite page: Fisher Ltd. for Dior, red unblocked felt hood with original label, 1955–65.

Long fluorescent tube lighting, placed in the same direction as the milliner's large worktable illuminates the workroom. Correct lighting plays a key part in the intricate processes involved in creating a hat. If a hat is being made for a catwalk show, it will be checked in the bright lights of the upstairs studio. If it is being made for a private client to wear at an event such as a wedding, it will be checked outside in the daylight. For every collection each milliner will be assigned four styles of hat to make. Two of the styles will relate to their specialist area and the other two will be, in Jones's words, 'more of a challenge'.

Production often involves starting work on several hats at a time, depending on orders. For example, a number of brims may be made before the crown of the hat is begun. The tools used by the milliners are simple – thimble, needles, cotton thread (synthetic threads have a slight stretch which is not suitable for hand-stitched hats), a medium pair of scissors and a small pair of scissors. In contrast, the actual fabrics and materials used in creating the hats are far more complex and varied.

Traditional materials such as straw and felt still form the backbone of the milliner's trade. Felt is made from fibres of fur or wool, compressed together. Historically beaver fur was used to make hat felt, and its popularity contributed to the establishment of the fur trade between America and Europe in the sixteenth century. But by the late nineteenth century beavers had been hunted into such small numbers that the trade began to use the soft fur from the underbelly of rabbits instead. Wool felt is formed from the short staples of wool which are unsuitable for weaving into cloth. Clement, third bishop of Rome and subsequently the patron saint of hatters, supposedly discovered how to make felt when, on a long journey, he put sheep's wool into his sandals to soften them. The combination of moisture (from perspiration) and pressure (the weight of his body) allegedly created felt. Traditionally the fibres used to make felt were softened with mercury, then shredded and formed into hoods on heated rounded copper cones, which were dampened to make the fibres adhere. The hoods passed through several shrinking processes in order to strengthen them. They were finally treated with shellac (a natural polymer secreted by Kerria insects, used as a varnish and glazing agent) before being sent to be blocked.

Above: Hats which have been exposed to mercury during production are stored in sealed bags within the Museum archives. A label with skull and cross bones denotes exposure to toxic material.

Opposite page: Sally Victor, collapsible straw hat, 1950s.

Many workers in the hat trade were affected by mercury poisoning, hence the phrase 'as mad as a hatter'. While there is minimal risk of contamination from handling mercury-treated hats, the V&A is obliged to take precautions with its own collection of felt hats. Each potentially mercury-treated hat is individually bagged in clear conservation plastic and marked with a 'toxic' label depicting a little skull and crossbones.

Straw hats can be made from paper, palm leaves or synthetic straw, but the traditional straw used in hat construction came from the stalks of rice and wheat. This straw needs to be bleached and split in preparation for weaving or braiding. However, fine straw from the Lombardy region of Italy was a premium material as it did not need splitting. The capital of Lombardy, Leghorn, gave its name to the popular 'Leghorn bonnets' of the nineteenth century. Straw was woven into long braids of different patterns, known as straw plait. The plait would then be carefully stitched together to form the hat. For many years *spartre* (a woven straw), was used to make the basic shape and support of structured fabric hats. The *spartre* would then be covered with the chosen material, attached by rubber solution glue or hand-stitching. Today rubber solution has been banned along with many other substances traditionally used in millinery, and *spartre* has been replaced with buckram, a stiffened grid-like fabric. PVC, latex, cut Perspex and vacuum-formed acrylic are some of the more contemporary materials used by Jones.

While new materials and innovations are constantly embraced within the discipline of millinery, the milliner's art also retains a respect and reverence for the traditions inherent to the practice. Deborah Miller refers to herself as 'the memory of Stephen Jones Millinery'. The pattern for each hat created in his workroom is placed in a box or file titled with the name of the milliner who created it. When a pattern is needed for reference or re-creation, it is Deborah who remembers the name of the particular milliner who made it (even several years after they may have left) and is then able to find the pattern. In Paris, St Catherine is the patron saint of dressmakers, and each year on St Catherine's day unmarried women over the age of 25 working in couture workrooms have been presented with a bonnet in the colours of St Catherine – yellow and green – and these traditions still remain strong. The hats would be made by fellow members of the workroom. Today at Christian Dior the hats are designed annually by Stephen Jones, who travels to Paris for the celebration to ensure that each Catherinette's hat is placed correctly on her head. The unmarried men are similarly presented with hats in the name of St Nicholas.

The making of the milliner

As he describes at the beginning of this book, Stephen Jones discovered millinery while working at the house of Lachasse on a summer placement from his fashion degree course at St Martin's School of Art. Here he learnt under the watchful eye of Shirley Hex, the head of the Lachasse millinery workroom. Jones graduated in fashion, but his training owed more to the traditional method of apprenticeship than to college studies as, at the time, there was no option to specialize in millinery at St Martin's.

Left: Christian Dior presents one of his atelier staff with a 'Catherinette' hat, 1957.

Opposite page: Galliano and Jones reinvented the Catherinette for the Dior *haute couture* show, autumn/winter 2005.

Millinery is a relatively modern profession, distinct from that of the hatmaker. While hats have been made and worn for many thousands of years, the rise of the milliner – maker of women's decorated and fashionable hats – is tied directly to the quickening pace of a consumer society and the emergence of the modern fashion system in the eighteenth century. The routes into becoming a milliner have always been many and varied. During the nineteenth century two years' apprenticeship was viewed as the standard millinery training, but in practice anyone so inclined could set themselves up as a milliner. The majority of milliners were women. As sewing was the basis of a girl's education, most women had good needleworking skills – the main requirement for proficiency in the trade. A Lady's maid was often required to be proficient at trimming hats in order to maintain her employer's wardrobe, and millinery skills could certainly improve employment prospects.

Apart from apprenticeship and being self-taught, those interested in learning the trade could also attend millinery schools. These were either private establishments or, from the beginning of the twentieth century, trade schools. 'The School of Millinery, 39 Ebury Street' was a private establishment in London, which advertised courses in *Queen* magazine in 1893 as being suitable for 'home purposes and to earn a living', with 'certificates of proficiency given to the successful'.[6]

The first half of the twentieth century was a prosperous period for the millinery trade, as every outfit required a matching hat. Etiquette deemed it essential to wear a hat out of doors, and within fashion circles the desire to be seen in new and exciting designs grew ever more competitive. The steady growth in the fashion industry meant that there was now internationally a demand for workers, which the apprenticeship system alone could not meet. In 1910 the *New York Times* reported on a meeting of the National Association of Retail Milliners, which resulted in a call for a 'College of Millinery Art' to be set up in the city in the realization that 'styles in millinery are closely associated with the healthy growth of a National Art'.[7]

In Britain, the London County Council Technical Education Board established trade schools, starting in 1915, to train pupils for industries that required skilled craft labour. During the previous year the Apprenticeship and Skilled Employment Association of London had published a comparative chart of expected earnings for those working in skilled trades, including what a milliner in a smart west-end millinery establishment could hope to earn: '2s week for the first year, 5s week 2nd, rising to 12–18s weekly when competent. Head of room 30s – £2 10s Weekly.'[8] To put this into context, in 1915 Harrods department store was retailing a lady's Panama hat at 18s 9d, and a smart three-cornered hat for daywear at 29s 6d.

«Mam'selle Coco, j'voudrais un beau chapeau pour le Dimanche»

By the end of the nineteenth century the attitude towards milliners had started to change, with millinery no longer seen as a purely working-class trade. Women had always been in the workplace, but by this time many middle-class women began to enter professional employment, particularly in America. Millinery became a popular career option for many women who wished to establish their own businesses. A number of well-known fashion designers began their careers as milliners at the end of the nineteenth century and the beginning of the twentieth. Jeanne Lanvin opened her Parisian millinery shop in 1889, Gabrielle Chanel set up her business in 1908 and Lucile in London – spurred on to support herself and her daughter by a divorce which left her in adverse circumstances – started her business in 1894.

Above: Sem (Georges Goursat), Gabrielle (Coco) Chanel as a milliner, from *Le grand Mode à l'Envers*, 1919.

Opposite page: Lucile, plaited straw hat decorated with velvet flowers, 1908. Worn by Miss Heather Firbank. V&A: T.117–1960.

Opposite page: Lilly Daché trying out a new design in her salon.

Below: Milliner Aage Thaarup learns how to make a palm leaf hat with 'Coconut Willy', a Honolulu-based hat maker who created ornately decorated sunhats all fashioned from palm leaves.

Right: James Wedge, hat of mustard yellow felt and black fringing, 1957. Designed for Liberty.

The gender distinction between milliners and hatmakers that had hitherto existed was also beginning to disappear. Traditionally milliners (makers of women's hats) were female while hatters (producers of men's hats) were male. However, by 1920 some of the most high-profile millinery designers were men. Milliners such as Benjamin B. Green-Field (1897–1989) of Bes-Ben in Chicago, Mr John (c.1902–93) and Frederic Hirst of John Frederics in New York, and Aage Thaarup (1906–87) in London demonstrated designing pieces that women longed to wear and own.

Apart from private millinery salons, employment was also available in the big department stores, which had busy millinery departments selling both ready-made and model millinery hats. The flamboyant New York milliner Lilly Daché (1898–1989; p.68) initially trained in Paris with Suzanne Talbot and Caroline Reboux, before moving to America in 1924 where she first found employment in the hat section at Macy's department store in New York. Her contemporary Sally Victor (1905–77) also began her millinery career in Macy's.

In 1948 the former fashion journalist Madge Garland (1898–1990) established the fashion school at London's Royal College of Art (the RCA). It was a significant matter that fashion, and therefore millinery, had become accepted as a relevant subject by the most important art school in Britain. Ten years on, fashion underwent a huge change of direction. Milliner James Wedge attended the two-year millinery course in the late 1950s. He was to become one of the stars of the fashion scene of 1960s London. He also represented a new generation of art school graduates whose education had been made possible by a new inclusive and progressive education system. Wedge opened his own millinery store in Soho in 1962, and he recalled: 'I used to put on my own collection twice a year. All the fashion people used to come and see it and they couldn't get in … so they used to sit on the staircase outside and wait until the others came out and ask what the hats were like!'[9]

Below: Stephen Jones's first hat made when he was an intern at the London couture house of Lachasse. The hat was submitted to Shirley Hex, the head of the millinery workroom.

By the late 1970s, millinery courses were being offered by a number of art and vocational schools. Deborah Miller trained at Medway College of Art and Design in Kent, and was first employed by the millinery house of Dolores. She recalls that it was staffed mostly by older women, with a smaller group of younger people. She was unique in having a college training. Her co-workers later told her that when she first arrived they all thought that she was related to the bosses, because she was given hats to do. They had had to work on linings before being allowed to progress to hats.[10]

Interestingly when Philip Treacy was an intern at Stephen Jones's Millinery, he noted that Deborah only ever gave him linings to make.

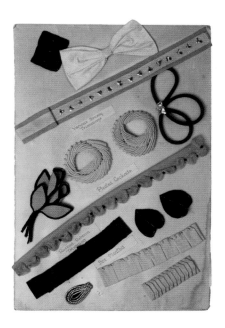

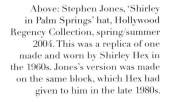

Above: Stephen Jones, 'Shirley in Palm Springs' hat, Hollywood Regency Collection, spring/summer 2004. This was a replica of one made and worn by Shirley Hex in the 1960s. Jones's version was made on the same block, which Hex had given to him in the late 1980s.

Above right: Millinery techniques illustrated with examples from a mid-twentieth-century millinery-making kit. Museum of London: 80.164.

Stephen Jones's tutor Shirley Hex (p.70) also supervised the millinery education of Philip Treacy, whom she taught at the RCA at the beginning of the 1990s. From his graduation onwards Treacy received great acclaim for his intricate and dramatic hats, often sculpted from feathers. In 1996 Suzy Menkes referred to him as 'a Brancusi of hatmakers, taking the head as a base for his fantastic sculptures'.[11] Shirley Hex has been a key figure in the revival and promotion of British millinery talent over the past 30 years. At Lachasse, as we have seen, she infused Stephen Jones with a passion for millinery. She later moved to head up the workroom at Frederick Fox, where the young Deborah Miller worked alongside her, and she was recruited by the RCA in the 1990s in order to establish its current millinery programme. Here she inspired and taught another generation of milliners, including Flora McLean and Noel Stewart. The respect in which her former students

hold her reflects her exacting standards and consummate technique. Her no-nonsense approach and her determination to encourage the highest skills and standards in her pupils could be summed up by her comment to a young Stephen Jones on his first day in the Lachasse millinery workroom: 'If your hands moved as fast as your mouth does, that hat would be finished by now!'[12]

Millinery is a trade that is constantly evolving and changing. Looking at a box of old millinery tools and fabrics in the Museum of London, Stephen Jones was surprised to find materials which he hadn't seen since the early days of his career and which are no longer being produced. Asked if he regretted the demise of such products, his reply was: 'Absolutely not, because there is always something else, something new to take its place'.[13]

Left: Justin Smith, pigskin top hat printed with bat motif, 2007.

Below: Nasir Mazhar, 'Cube' hat for Gareth Pugh, spring/summer 2008.

Opposite page: Singer Beyoncé on the cover of *The Face* magazine, wearing a rubber beret by House of Flora, October 2003.

Today London remains the creative centre of the millinery world, with two of the most highly regarded contemporary milliners – Stephen Jones and Philip Treacy – based in the city. London is also home to important makers, such as Prudence who designs for Vivienne Westwood, and a younger generation of milliners such as Nasir Mazhar and Noel Stewart. Recent graduates of the RCA such as Justin Smith and Søren Bach, ensure that the city's millinery success is assured to continue well into the future.

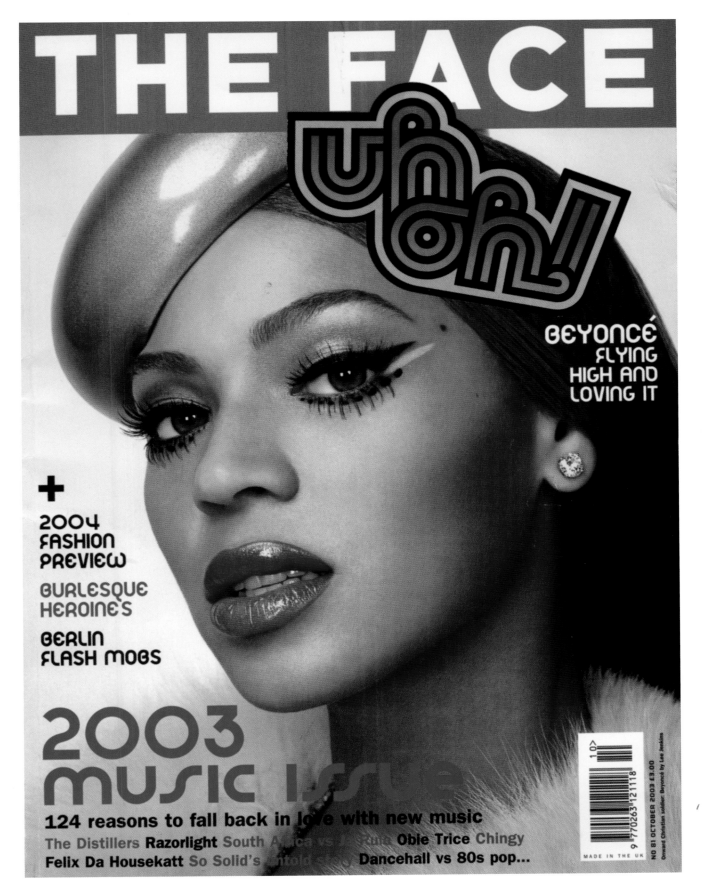

THE FACE

uh oh!

BEYONCÉ
FLYING
HIGH AND
LOVING IT

+

2004
FASHION
PREVIEW

BURLESQUE
HEROINES

BERLIN
FLASH MOBS

2003
music issue

124 reasons to fall back in love with new music

The Distillers Razorlight South Africa vs Berlin Oble Trice Chingy
Felix Da Housekatt So Solid's untold story Dancehall vs 80s pop...

NO 81 OCTOBER 2003 £3.00
Onward Christian soldier: Beyoncé by Lee Jenkins

9 770263 121118
MADE IN THE UK

THE HATBOX

Many of the hats in the V&A archives were donated or acquired along with their original boxes. Stephen Jones was delighted to find that a 1950s brown-and-white striped hatbox, from the milliner Rudolf, had been made by the firm Thomas Norman – today they supply Jones' own signature octagonal hatboxes.

Hatboxes come in many different forms but can be divided into two distinct types. Sturdy luggage pieces were intended both for travelling and long-term storage, while the more decorative and ephemeral boxes were most often supplied by the milliner.

Originally hatboxes were created to allow felt hats to be safely transported. The ardours of travel required a sturdy casing for such an object, which could be easily damaged. A seventeenth-century hatbox in the collection of the V&A is fashioned from leather and card, and follows the silhouette of the tall wide-brimmed felt hat for which it was made. Lacquered tin cases also became popular as a safe way of transporting hats, particularly those worn in an official capacity such as the bicorns worn by the military or members of the Royal court. These also closely followed the line of the hat in their construction. For women, bonnet boxes – small structured cases often woven from wicker with a small handle on top – offered a light, practical way to transport their bonnets.

Top left: Hatboxes from the V&A archives, from department store Marshall and Snelgrove and milliners Rudolf and Aage Thaarup.

Top right: William Marshall Craig, *Buy a Bonnet Box*, 1804, V&A: E.857-2000.

Opposite: 'Joan with a hat' by Jean Barthet, Paris 1953.

In *The Glass of Fashion* Cecil Beaton remembered the luggage of his stylish aunt, recalling: Then there were the hatboxes – great square containers that held six hats apiece. In those days mesh moulds were pinned on the sides top and bottom of a box so that the crown of the hat could be placed over the mould and fixed into place by a long hat pin piercing the mesh. In such a manner six hats could travel in a box without being crushed.

The increasingly sophisticated trade in fancy goods and accessories during the eighteenth century highlighted the importance of attractive packaging to the consumer. Accessories such as fans and hats were sold with card boxes covered in decorative printed or painted paper. Numerous eighteenth-century engravings and paintings depict milliners with their decorated elongated hatboxes of card, transporting their wares through the streets or presenting their merchandise to customers from the box.

The V&A holds a gold-and-cream bonnet from 1890 from London-based milliner Mrs Ritchie. The matching hatbox is of a drum shape, with a printed milliner's label. It is a typical example of a hatbox from the period, and illustrates how the hatbox that we know today has changed little in the past century.

In Tony Richardson's 1961 film *A Taste of Honey*, set in the gritty reality of post-war northern Britain, The film draws on an identifiable scenario of how an object can inspire hope. An impoverished mother and daughter do a flit from their lodgings to avoid paying rent. Their worldly possessions consist of just two suitcases, a budgerigar in a cage and a stylish striped hatbox from the milliner Rudolf – a symbol of the mother's ever-hopeful outlook that a glamorous life is just around the corner.

JEAN BARTHET

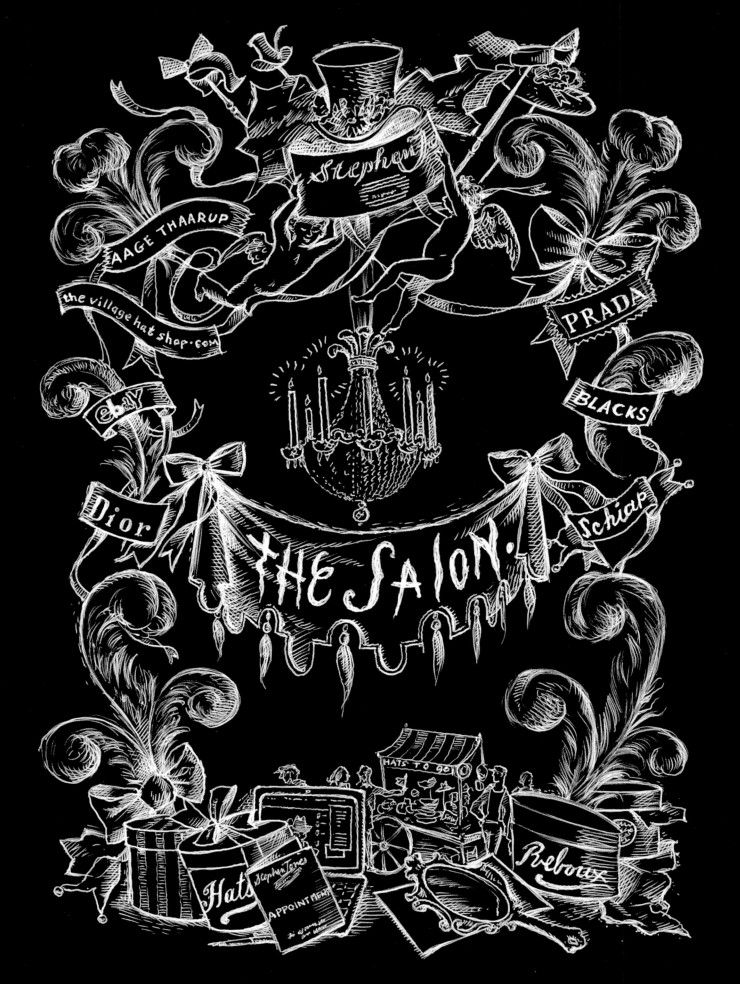

From the workroom the hats in the next step of their evolution go to the salon. The concept of the millinery salon is often even more engaging than the hats themselves. Banks of hats line the walls, each one different in colour, fabric and attitude. There are hatboxes and perfumed tissue paper. The experience is a lucky dip of fashion and style, each hat evoking times, moods and temperaments. From Rose Bertin's 1773 millinery shop, Au Grand Mogol, to the www.villagehatshop.com nowadays, the place where a hat is purchased is a large part of the hat's mystique. More esoteric and mysterious than a fashion shop, hats are an unknown quantity and not a daily purchase. However, once the person puts the hat on it becomes the focal point of the outfit; the hat explains your Look. But you see hats everywhere, not only in a salon. From the fashion journal the *Galeries des Modes* in 1776 to *i-D* magazine today, and from the first fashion show invented by Lucile at the end of the nineteenth century to shows of Gareth Pugh, hats have featured as a focal point to identify the Look. It may be ethnic, colourful, city, floral, funky, sexy, sportif, controversial, glamorous. Whether in my tiny shop in London or in the grandeur of the Dior salons in Paris, the hats tell a story unlike any other. Where clothes hang simply on a rail, hats whisper to the clients, 'try me on, I'm beautiful'.

Stephen Jones

The model millinery business is one of the very few international businesses that has changed little over the past hundred years. Customers' experience of millinery shops and the buying and selling of hats, occurs in two stages. The first, outside the shop, revolves around the lure of hats, experienced not just from looking through the window, but also from magazines, stores, films or the internet. It is the momentary glimpse in which the customer is hooked and driven to pursue their hat. It lies in capturing the imagination and fantasies of the customer, while also assuring them that their choice will inspire admiration in the onlooker. The second stage occurs inside the shop, in the salon – the physical act of purchasing within the specialized environment.

The slim eighteenth-century shop front of Stephen Jones's Covent Garden shop (see below), sits like a jewel amongst a row of stores and pubs, its discreet allure suggesting to the passer-by that they have discovered something unique, enticing them to ring the bell and enter down the red carpet which runs from the door through the length of the shop. Retaining its original architectural features, the salon is painted in Jones' signature lilac wash and furnished with miniature white dressing-tables, mirrors and mannequin heads. Behind the shop sit the showroom for private clients and the offices.

Left: Fashion plate depicting hat fashions for the year 1788. By the second half of the eighteenth century fashion plates were increasingly accessible, published in almanacs, pocket books (a form of diary) and in publications such as *Lady's Magazine* and *Galeries des Modes*.

Below left: Stephen Jones, 'HQ' hat, Covent Garden Collection, autumn/ winter 2008.

Below right: Façade of Stephen Jones Millinery, Covent Garden.

Opposite page: Auguste Macke, *Hatshop*, 1914. Folkwang Museum, Essen.

The millinery shop is a magical place, the site of transformation. Today, no longer the staple of every high street, the millinery store has become a specially sought-out destination – whether Stephen Jones Millinery in Covent Garden, Philip Treacy's salon in London's Belgravia, or the hat shop of Japanese brand CA4LA across town in Shoreditch, these places radiate an allure. The colourful window displays comprise an array of objects for any and everyone, regardless of size or age. Inside, the hats are displayed on stands, accessible for the client to examine and to touch, enticing the customer to try them on and to see how they will change their attitude and self-perception.

In the last quarter of the nineteenth century, many artists were drawn to painting everyday scenes of urban life. Amongst these modern subjects, previously considered unworthy of the attention of great painters, the milliner's shop was a popular theme. Renoir, Degas, Tissot, Henry Tonks and Paul Signac were among those who were drawn to paint women in the process of buying or trying on a hat. The atmosphere of the milliner's shop was akin to the boudoir, with its air of intimacy and femininity, yet it remained within the public sphere. The female customer, seduced by a beautiful hat, would be seated in front of a mirror as though at her dressing-table, and a physical interaction between the milliner and the customer would ensue as the former arranged the hat on the head of the latter. In most millinery shops, with their large window displays, this could all be openly observed by the passer-by, yet, in the painted depictions, the subjects are oblivious to the artist's gaze, giving a frisson of voyeurism to viewers of the painting.

Below: Marianne Topham, *Philip Treacy's Belgravia Hat Shop*, 1994. Museum of London: 94.21.

Right: Hilaire Germain Edgar Degas, *At the Millinery Shop*, 1884–90. Art Institute of Chicago. Degas' observation of a woman in a millinery store depicts her engrossed in trying on a hat.

Opposite page: Interior of Madame Suzy's millinery store in Paris. Cover of *Vogue*, illustrated by René Bouché, 1939.

Above: Madame Suzy, red-and-white woven straw with red veil, *c*.1937. V&A: T.62–1967.

The millinery experience could also be enjoyed within the grand spaces of the department store, where the millinery section was often a sumptuous and enticing space. The imposing New York department store Hugh O'Neill's, which opened in 1887 occupying a full block of Sixth Avenue, was one such example:

> The Millinery department, on the second floor at the 21st street corner, was a showpiece with gilded columns. The ceiling and wall were finished in Japanese paper, and there was a cornice of ebony latticework with colored glass. In the corner, a banquette ran around a circular window – the nook was partly secluded by hangings of silk tapestry.[1]

No expense had been spared to create a lavish environment in which women were enticed to buy their hats.

Aside from department stores and small independent shops, there were the exclusive, mostly Paris-based salons that were run along the same lines as the couture system (outlined in 'Creation'), with a *vendeuse* (sales woman) assigned to each customer. Access to these exclusive salons was no easy matter. Historian Bianca M. du Mortier explains in her book *Chapeau, Chapeaux!* that admittance to Parisian salons was only possible through the mediation of an existing client, who had to recommend her friend or acquaintance to a *vendeuse*. Du Mortier goes on to say that the client generally made her choice on the first visit. Once the order was placed, the client then made two more visits for fittings.[2]

Salons were run on a very hierarchical basis, where often only the most loyal or favoured customers would be allowed to see the full range of available hats. Wealthy American buyers in France often complained that they were treated as second-class customers, regardless of what they spent. A *New York Times* reporter in Paris in 1914 noted:

> These designers know just to whom to show certain hats. They know who should not be let into the inner rooms. You can tell by the location you are given just what your value is to the premier *vendeuse*. And it is not always a question of money: some of those who buy most lavishly are not allowed a peep into the mysteries that are kept for those, who, knowing much, refuse to buy unless they are treated with distinction.[3]

The idea of national differences and style in millinery was another issue that preoccupied style observers and fashion commentators. In the 1930s Mrs C.W. Forester wrote that, 'The majority of Englishwomen do not attach nearly enough importance to the selection of their headgear. They buy in a casual and haphazard manner, all unworthy of the solemn issues involved in the purchase'.[4] The Englishwoman's disinterest in hat-buying was made all the worse in comparison to their cross-channel contemporaries. 'A Frenchwoman', Forester primly noted, 'seldom makes this mistake'. The Woman's Institute seconded this perceived sophistication: 'Perfect millinery is a matter of much concern with the French, who not only possess a true appreciation of style, but also insist on perfection of detail and consummate effect'.[5] Paris was the centre of the fashion world at this time, and as such the general consensus was that a Frenchwoman would naturally have more flair and style when it came to the issue of hats.

THE MILLINERY SALONS AT HARRODS.

Opposite page: Hat illustrations by Francis Marshall, 1950. Francis Marshall was a regular visitor to the Paris fashion shows, where he sketched the latest looks to accompany fashion articles written by Iris Ashley in the *Daily Mail*.

Left: Harrods millinery department, 1911

This is for usual Friday Feature (August 4th)
Cut
Sent to Process
31/7/50

Opposite: Interior of Mr John's millinery salon, New York, c.1960.

Right: Milliner Madame Agnès pictured with furniture and interior design Jean Dunand, who was responsible for the design of the ultra-modern interior of her millinery salon.

Below: Interior of Lilly Daché's millinery salon, New York, 1930s.

The millinery salon was a key destination for every stylish woman of the early twentieth century, and the design of the interior was a crucial part of creating an environment to add to the experience of the purchase. In 1920s Paris, one of the most elegant millinery shops was the salon of Agnès, a milliner who had trained with Reboux and gone on to open her own highly successful business. Her salon was designed by the artist and designer Jean Dunand (1877–1942). A close friend of Agnès, Dunand was known for his lacquer furniture, and he created a clean modern space as the perfect backdrop to the stylish minimal cloche hats for which Agnès was known.

Some of the most elaborate and outrageous millinery salons opened in New York in the mid-twentieth century. The emphasis was on creating an atmosphere where the customer was drawn into the imaginary world of the milliner, leaving reality outside at the door. Lilly Daché, who built her eight-storey 'House of Hats' just off Park Avenue in 1937, had a silver fitting-room for brunette celebrities and a gold one for blondes, as well as a specially padded pink satin room with a leopard-skin divan for buyers.[6] To 1930s clients this opulent interior echoed the glamour and excess of the cinematic world. The celebrated New York and Hollywood milliner Mr John, formerly of John Frederics, opened his own Manhattan salon in the 1950s (opposite). Lavishly decorated with Louis XVI-style fixtures and fittings, draped with red velvet curtains and littered with ceramic figures and animals, it was an exercise in kitsch flamboyance, a fantastical space that guaranteed the customers a unique experience.

Above: Interior of Biba shop on Kensington Church Street, London, with hatstands, and 'mountie' hat on display, c.1966–9.

Opposite page: Steve's Chapeau Boo-tique, part of Stephen Jones retrospective exhibition, Dover Street Market, London, 2005

In the 1960s certain rules of etiquette gradually broke down. Extreme hair fashions were one manifestation of change and were a blow for the millinery trade. Many shops closed their doors. However, at the same time, a new audience was being introduced to the process of buying hats through London's ultra-fashionable Biba store (see above) – which produced fast fashion at affordable prices, all stylishly displayed on its signature bent-wood hat-stands. For the Biba girl, the hat was the ultimate accessory, and the store stocked 'hats for all ages, occasions and eventualities'.[7]

The formalized fashionable silhouette of the 1980s and the return to 'dressing up' provided a real boost to the millinery industry. In this positive climate, Carole and Nigel Denford had the idea of establishing 'The Hat Shop' in London's Covent Garden, encouraging hat wearers to return to the salon environment and the personal experience of buying a hat to suit the wearer. Their own range of hats covered 'virtually every aspect of headwear from everyday street fashion through partywear to hats suitable for the most formal occasion'.[8] They also stocked hats from a diverse group of young milliners, including Fred Bare, Jo Buckley, Misa Harada and Rachel Trevor Morgan. When it first opened, the Hat Shop attracted queues outside the door every Saturday.

Today the internet has become the new marketplace for fashion, and while many general on-line fashion stores sell hats, specific millinery sites such as www.villagehatshop.com are increasingly popular. In a sense this experience replicates that of the millinery shop window – attracting and alerting the passer-by or browsers to a hat. The window-shopping experience precludes the touching and trying of the hat, but the importance of the exercise is that it has captured the attention of the customer and at the touch of a button the hat can be summoned. What cannot be replicated, however, is the actual experience of trying on numerous hats while receiving the advice of experts, whose sole purpose is to ensure the right hat for the right customer.

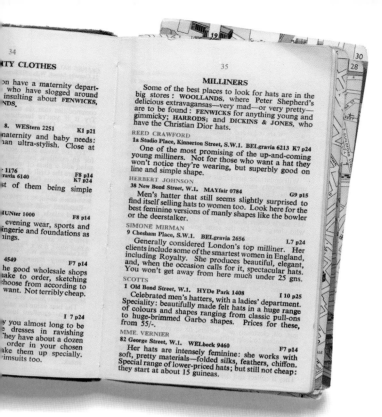

Opposite page: The young Halston places a hat on the head of actress Anita Colby at Bergdorf Goodman department store, New York, 1965.

Above: Sheila Chichester, *London Women*, 1957.

At Stephen Jones Millinery the customer is encouraged to try as many styles as she likes, while the *vendeuse* Cornelia offers advice on particular styles which may suit and correct ways of wearing and angling a hat. This advice is invaluable to the customer. Choosing a hat is not always a straightforward matter, and can be a stressful occasion for those unsure of what they want. Hats are not a neutral accessory, and can be a revealing statement about the wearer. Traditionally much was invested in the choice of hat. The wrong selection could invite public ridicule, and as such the advice of the milliner or *vendeuse* was paramount. Jean Rhys drew on this aspect of customer care in her novel, *Good Morning, Midnight*. Sasha Jensen, the tragic protagonist, appeals to a milliner for help with her purchase when buying a hat:

'You know I'm bewildered, please tell me which one I ought to have.'
'The first one I showed you' she says at once.
'Oh my God, not that one.'
'Or perhaps the third one.'
When I put on the third one she says: 'I don't want to insist, but yes – that is your hat.' Assured by the milliner's decisiveness, Sasha notes 'I feel saner and happier after this'.[9]

This physical transformation is inevitably closely linked with an emotional one. The morale-boosting properties of purchasing a new hat are less noted today, but in the past the importance of the ritual was readily recognized. In his autobiography, milliner Aage Thaarup quoted a 1936 *News Chronicle* article by the journalist Jane Gordon: 'If I were a psycho-analyst I would go into partnership with a really smart milliner. Because if I knew my job as a psycho-analyst, I would realize that most inhibitions and repressions that afflict the modern woman could be cured quite simply by a new hat.'[10]

In the new millennium, the idea of niche marketing and luxury branding caused fashion to abandon the mass market and seek out ever-exclusive experiences to entice customers. The milliner's salon could be viewed as the epitome of this stance. What could be more exclusive than the sumptuous environs of the milliner's shop, with its one-on-one service and stock of unique and exquisitely handmade pieces, all for less than the cost of a mass-produced handbag of the season? In a climate of stealth luxury, a model hat does not advertise a label or fashion house – although those in the know may recognize the style of the milliner – but the hat will serve to mark out the individuality of the wearer and separate her from the crowd.

THE TURBAN

The turban is a headdress created from wrapped and folded fabric. Historically associated with India, it has many different cultural and social connotations, in different parts of the world. It often defines religious affiliations and status. Traditionally the turban was an item of men's dress, with different styles, shapes and fabrics worn by different cultural groups – such as male Sikhs, for whom the wearing of a turban is one aspect of denoting their affiliation.

In western fashion, turbans have mostly been worn by women. While at times it has been a more prominent element of fashion, the turban has remained a constant element of women's fashionable dress throughout the past three hundred years.

The serious commercial exchange which grew up with the establishment of the East India Company from the late sixteenth century led to a proliferation of items – such as shawls, printed cottons and silks – being appropriated into western fashion. By the early eighteenth century, figures such as Lady Mary Wortley-Montague, the well-travelled wife of an English diplomat, started a vogue for the wearing of eastern dress and turbans in portraiture. The style of dress was seen as a reference to the exotic harems of the east, but also regarded as a timeless style which did not date as quickly as fashionable clothing.

By 1800 the turban was part of mainstream fashion, and numerous fashion plates portray figures with their heads wrapped and draped in imaginatively styled turbans with fanciful names. By the 1820s the fashionable turban had developed from a wrapped piece of fabric into a more elaborate construction, in a variety of padded and embellished fabrics. One such piece in the collection of the V&A is a sumptuous arrangement of tartan silk interspersed with black velvet banding.

For most of the Victorian era, connotations of the harem and be-trousered women caused the turban to be relegated to artistic circles, but the early twentieth century ushered in its return as a chic form of evening headdress. The designer Paul Poiret (1879–1944) laid claim to its introduction, but the popularity of the style owed much to the exotically attired dancers of Diaghilev's Ballets Russes, which became the toast of Paris in 1909. Poiret recalled how his turbans were inspired by a trip to the V&A:

I visited the South Kensington Museum ... There I found the most precious documents relative to Indian art and manners. In particular there was a collection of turbans that enchanted me ... I admired unwearyingly the diversity of their so logical and so elegant forms ... I at once obtained from the Keeper permission to work from these magnificent specimens ... I immediately telegraphed to Paris for one of my premières ... and she spent eight days in the Museum, imitating and copying, reproducing the models she had before her eyes: a few weeks later we had made turbans the fashion in Paris. (*My First Fifty Years*, Paul Poiret, London, 1931)

Often decorated with precious stones or feathers affixed to the centre, the fashionable turban was reunited with trousers when sumptuous silk pyjamas became the ultimate in 1920's evening and at-home wear.

Opposite page: Paul Poiret
turban by Georges Lepape
(1887–1971), hand-coloured pochoir
les choses de Paul Poiret, 1911.

Below: Prada turban,
spring/summer, 2006.

Above right: Clementine
Churchill wearing a silk scarf
turban with her husband, Sir
Winston, in 1990.

This easy and comfortable style was adopted as beachwear in the 1930s, protecting hair from the elements while containing it in a stylish manner. During the Second World War, the turban was a popular garment for its practical properties, restraining the hair while in the workplace but also allowing a nod to fashion, easily created from a length of left-over fabric or a scarf – an important factor in a time of fabric rationing. In solidarity with working women, Winston Churchill's wife Clementine took to wearing a scarf wrapped around her head. In Paris, turbans reached controversial heights in the pieces created by Parisian *modistes*, who sought to bait the German authorities with their flouting of fabric restrictions. The German authorities were unimpressed by the increasingly dramatic and exaggerated forms being worn by fashionable women, and warned head of *haute couture*, Lucien Lelong, the head of the Chambre Syndicale de Haute Couture (the body in charge of organizing and promoting the French Fashion Industry), that restrictions must be observed. However the style was impossible to police, as many women could create their own dramatic versions with remnants of fabric.

In the post-war period the turban remained a fashionable style, but worn small and styled tightly to the head, it bore little resemblance to the outlandish war-time versions. The Parisian milliner Madame Paulette (1900–1974) was known for her skill in creating turbans. Whether simple draped silks or more complex pieces worked around a net base, she created endless permutations including a red silk jersey turban worn by ballerina Margot Fonteyn and now in the collection of the Museum of Fashion in Bath.

By the 1970s the turban had been reintroduced as an important accessory in a retrospective vogue for 1940s style. From Parisian couturier Yves Saint Laurent (1937–2008) to London retailer Barbara Hulanicki of Biba, the turban was the most elegant headwear to sport. With the emergence of the streetstyle of the New Romantics in the 1980s the turban had yet another revival, worn by both men and women, and later in the decade it was a popular women's sports choice worn in different fabrics as a thick band for skiing and beachwear. In 2006 Prada reinstated the turban as a high-fashion hat when they sent bright jewel covered versions down their spring/summer catwalk.

A hat is nothing until worn. When a brim shadows an eye seductively, or a feather exaggerates the movement of the head, this is when all the effort put into the hat has meaning. The wearer brings the hat alive, whether it is for running an errand on a rainy January afternoon or a First Lady getting off a plane in front of reporters. The hat's impact is a synthesis of who the person is and who they want to be. When the two are blended together it becomes a great personal signature. Of course this is the hallmark of the iconic hat wearers of our time, from Madonna to Her Majesty the Queen Mother. Like the designer, they want a dream, an evocation of beauty, glamour and elegance. But clients bring their own ideas too – a major statement for a particular occasion or a hat for everyday, a brimmed hat for the sun or a hat that can be squashed so it can travel. A hat that is inexpensive. Light hats that can be worn all day, and hats for bad hair days too.

For me, collaborating with clients is an adventure whether they are a bridesmaid from Lancashire or Rei Kawakubo preparing for a fashion show. There is never a formula and every time is like the first time. From the original concept through to the making and fitting of the hat, I always think the hat is not finished until either the end of that wedding reception or until the last model comes off the catwalk. Only then I can relax, until the next time...

Stephen Jones

When the right hat meets the right client, the performance of wearing begins. Clients or wearers represent the final stage in the life cycle of a hat, bringing the headgear out into the wider world and revealing it for all to see. One of Stephen Jones' most noted clients is Italian fashion editor Anna Piaggi (b.1931), who has been wearing his hats since the 1980s. Regularly photographed in the front row of the international catwalk shows, Piaggi stands out from the crowd in her colourful ensembles, always topped off with a Stephen Jones hat. Jones is quoted as saying, 'The thing about making hats for her is it's a frame for her face. There's a lightness of spirit. My hats cheer her up'.[1] While Jones is very much involved in the world of high fashion, there is no one typical client, just as there is no one typical hat. From a mother-of-the-bride or a customer seeking a hat for the races at Ascot, to a well-known celebrity or a designer client, Jones deals with every kind of remit and millinery challenge.

Every client has a unique approach to wearing their hats. Often they will be faithful to one particular milliner. Just as Anna Piaggi is known for her Stephen Jones hats, so Isabella Blow (1958–2007) was the muse for Philip Treacy, and Gertrude Shilling (1910–99) wore only the hats of her son, milliner David Shilling. Philip Treacy first met with fashion editor Isabella Blow as a student, when he went to pick up one of his hats from the offices of *Tatler* magazine and was introduced to 'this very striking and slightly intimidating woman'.[2] Treacy subsequently received a telephone call from Blow asking him to make her wedding hat. He recalled that Blow's patronage was driven by a combination of trust and instinct: 'I was only a student, just starting out and people kept saying to her "You're the fashion editor of *Tatler* – you could have anyone in the world, why get a student to do it?" But she didn't care … she trusted me.'[3] Blow wore Treacy's creations with an extraordinary style and confidence, whether it was an exquisite feather galleon or her name spelt out in white feathers, hovering above her face. The hats became an extension of herself, with no visible means of knowing where one ended and the other began.

Left: Anna Piaggi, wearing a Stephen Jones Union Jack top hat, Victoria and Albert Museum, London, 2006.

Opposite page: Isabella Blow, in a Philip Treacy hat, 1996. Through her patronage of Philip Treacy and her own dramatic be-hatted appearance, Isabella Blow sparked a renewed interest in millinery in the 1990s.

Gertrude Shilling, one of Britain's most noted and noticed hat wearers, known for her outrageous headgear (left), placed total confidence in her son David Shilling. Her extravagant, whimsical and oversized creations were an annual feature at Ascot. They included a gigantic apple with a large arrow through it, a layered Christmas tree and a large striped mushroom. She recalled one year how her hat was too big to allow her to fit through the door of their Rolls Royce: 'It was a scream. We had to ring ten car hire firms before we found one big enough. There were queues of cars blocking the street. As they arrived David would dash out and measure them up'.[4]

Other clients are noted for their devotion to a particular style of hat. The elegant ensembles worn by America's First Lady, Jacqueline Kennedy (1929–94), were frequently finished off with a pill-box hat. She adopted this easy, off-the-face style because she disliked wearing hats. While she wore early versions by Givenchy and Balenciaga, she later came to rely on the designer Roy Halston Frowick (1932–90), then milliner at New York department store Bergdorf Goodman.

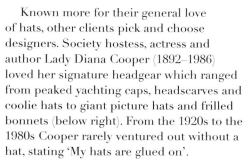

Known more for their general love of hats, other clients pick and choose designers. Society hostess, actress and author Lady Diana Cooper (1892–1986) loved her signature headgear which ranged from peaked yachting caps, headscarves and coolie hats to giant picture hats and frilled bonnets (below right). From the 1920s to the 1980s Cooper rarely ventured out without a hat, stating 'My hats are glued on'.

Today, American Burlesque performer Dita Von Teese (b.1974, p. 100) has a special room in her house dedicated to her own hat collection. As long as the style is right, she says she is just as happy to wear an unlabelled vintage hat as the latest couture creation. While she has access to the most exclusive hats and often wears spectacular headpieces for her performances, her favourite hat is an unlabelled 1940s white felt with a stuffed parrot perched on the crown. Hats have also played a key role in the image of many contemporary musicians, from Madonna to Mary J. Blige and Missy Elliott (p. 101); alongside defining style, hats are often a useful performance plot.

The joy at finding the right hat to suit your face, the confidence instilled by sporting the right headwear for a particular occasion, and the inherent possibilities of transformation, are all qualities to be enjoyed by the hat-wearer.

Opposite page: Dita Von Teese in
a veiled 1940s hat, 2008

Below: Missy Elliott wearing a hat
by Stephen Jones for Dior, 2004.

The right hat for the right client for the right occasion?

Throughout the first half of the twentieth century, the choice of hat was crucial to one's fashion credentials. Writing in 1956, Alison Adburgham emphasized the centrality of the hat's role in fashion: 'More than anything else this year it is the hats which confer the look of the season. They are very, very important. They are more significant than the dresses on which they set the seal…'[5] Hitting the message home, the article underlined how integral the hat was to the total look. The emphasis on the correct way of dressing sparked enough concern amongst the fashionable female population to provide a booming market for books on the etiquette of dress, published in their hundreds throughout the first half of the twentieth century.

Containing all manner of information on how to attire oneself correctly, the books would often dedicate a specific chapter to the hat, with the clear message that a woman's choice of millinery figured prominently in the impression she made on others. Advice varied from straightforward descriptions of how the line and proportion of a hat must suit both the individual and the occasion, to a more scientific approach involving tables of events and styles of dress and types of hats to be selected. For business, shopping or travelling the recommendation was 'a simple becoming hat harmonizing with dress, suit or coat: smartness and serviceability equally desirable', whereas for a church, club meeting or informal lunch the requirement was 'distinctive type: more elegant than for business wear but not over-elaborate'. An evening at home called for a 'bandeau or hair ornament, if desired, when entertaining'.[6] In hat-terms, all aspects of life and dress were covered.

Above: Novelist Dame Barbara Cartland was known for her love of pink and her extravagant hats. She was a client of milliner Frederick Fox.

Opposite page: Björk performing in a dramatic fur hat by Søren Bach, London, 2008.

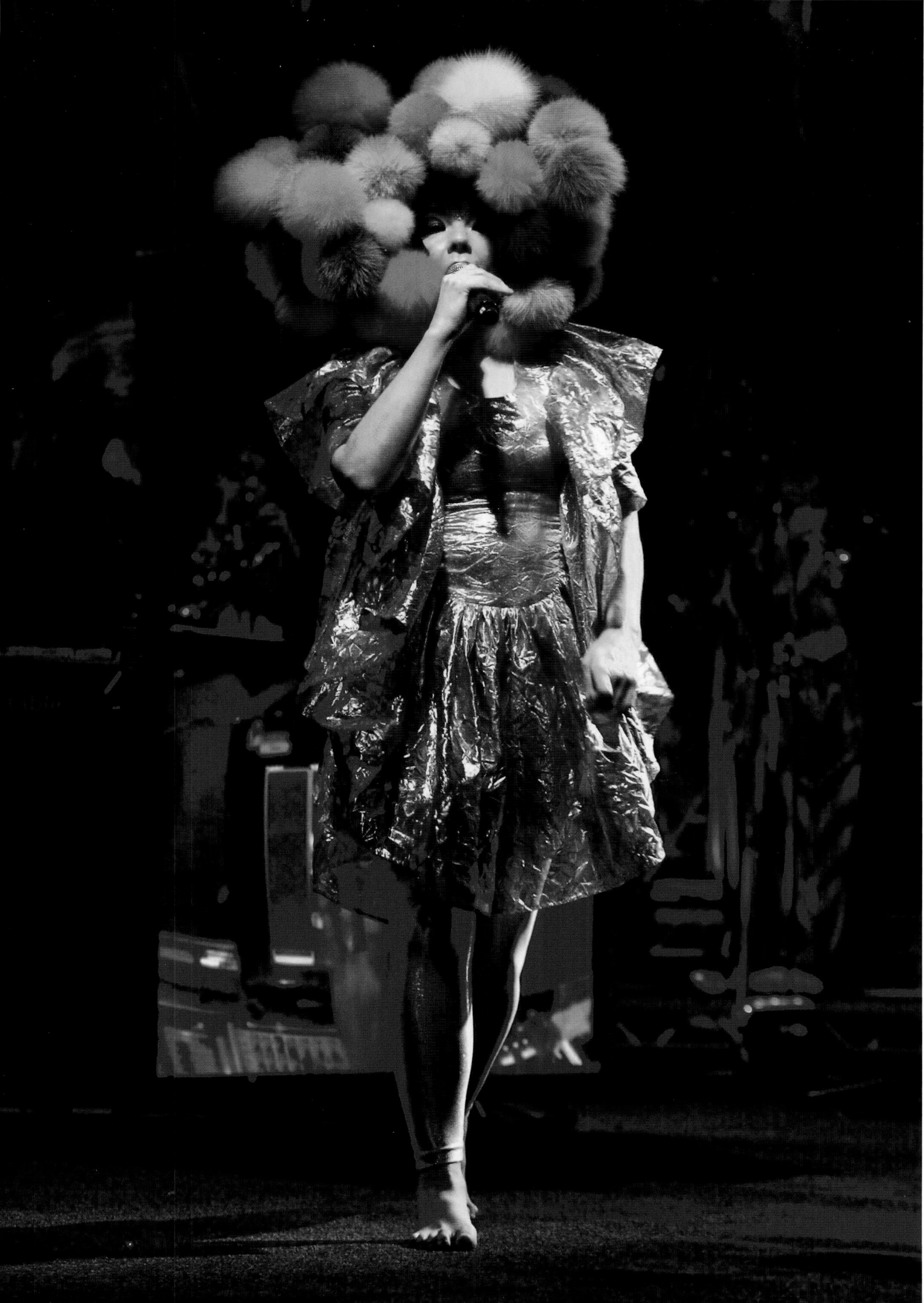

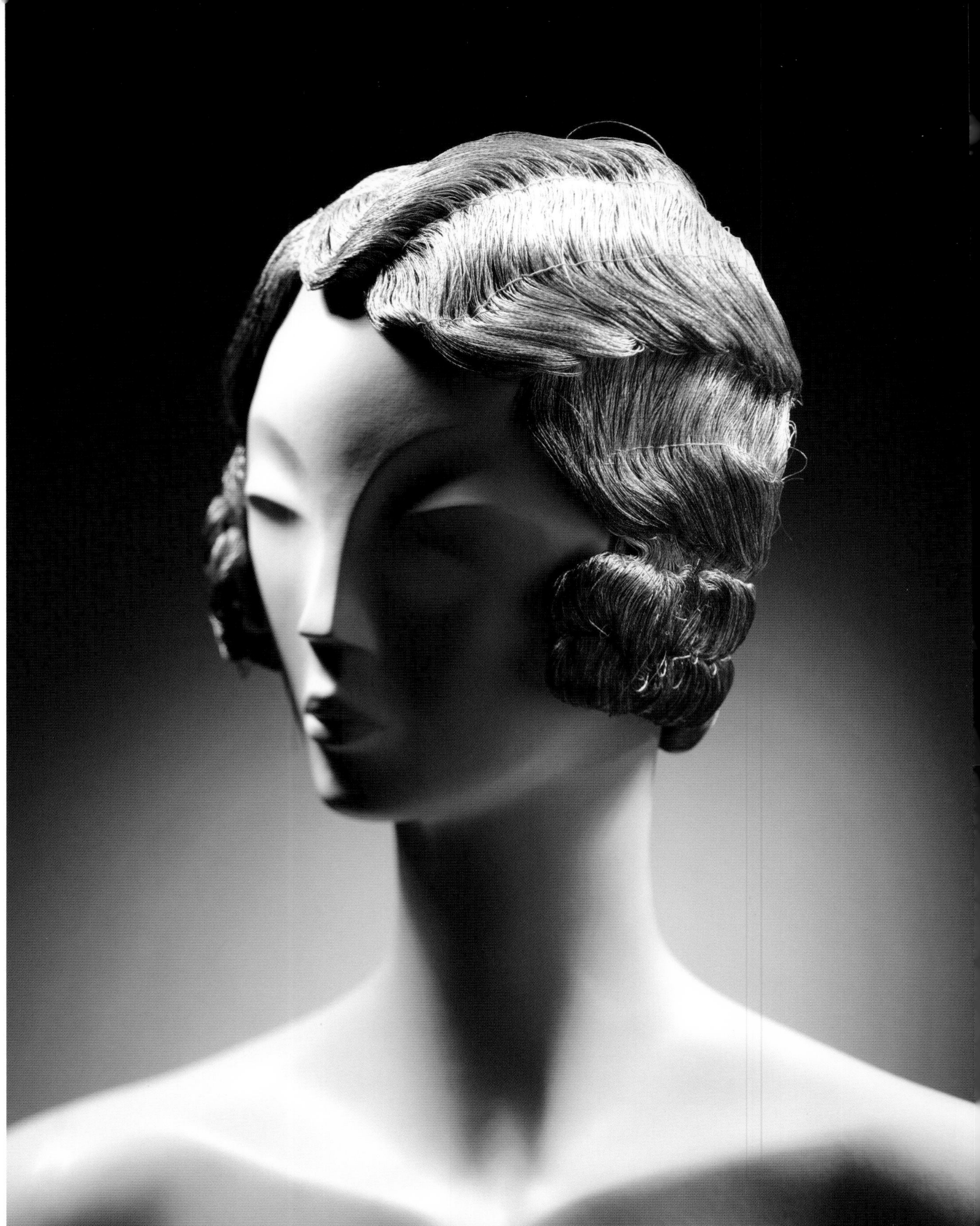

Opposite page: Unknown maker/
unlabelled, metallic thread silver
wig, 1922. Coloured wigs were
a popular choice for evening
headgear in the 1920s.
V&A: T.103A–1949.

Above: Stephen Jones, 'Roxette'
plastic wig hat, North Collection,
autumn/winter 2002.

While etiquette manuals advised
the personal client on hats to suit their
individual features, hat-wearing is also
dependent on a key factor – hairstyle. While
at times hats and hairstyles have warred
over the right to crown women's heads,
the symbiosis between the two is evident.
From the upswept cushioning hairstyles
that supported the vast hats of the early
twentieth century to the close-fitting cloche
hats of the 1920s, which required the hair
below to be cropped, bobbed or shingled,
their co-dependence is undeniable.
Stephen Jones recognizes this point, stating
that 'there would be no hats without hair'[7]
(instantly conceding exceptions while
running a hand over his own smooth and
hairless crown). The milliner needs to
work with, rather than against, the client's
hairstyle. Some milliners have even taken
the hair as inspiration. The 1920's vogue
for 'wig' evening hats is represented in the
collections of the V&A by a silver metallic
wig, each strand of silver thread carefully
arranged into a delicate shimmering
coiffure (p.104). The structured hats of the
1960s, perched on top of the head, echoed
the lines of the voluminous, set hairstyles,
while the silhouette of the vertical toque
hats of the 1980s found parallels in the
fashionable close-cropped and spiked hair
of the period. Jones himself has played with
the notion of hat as hair or hair as hat, his
multicoloured 'Roxette' wig hat of 2002
offering the client a chance to experience
long flowing locks of cellophane (above).

Summary of Milliners

Coquette	Sophisticate	Romantic	Patrician	Gamine	Exotic
Agnes	Agnes	Agnes		Schiaparelli	Alix
	Schiaparelli	Alix	Talbot		Reboux
Talbot	Reboux			Suzy	
	Suzy		Guy	Guy	
Thaarup	Thaarup	Thaarup	Bragaard	Thaarup	Thaarup
	Bragaard		Descat		
	Miss Ware		Miss Ware		Teddy Thompson
Teddy Thompson	Teddy Thompson				

Changing needs

At the beginning of the twentieth century, the growing popularity of sports amongst the female population led to a burgeoning market in sports hats and outfits. These new clients were separate from those who sought fashionable hats, but were no less stylish. A lady's motoring hat in the V&A collections is made from black and russet coloured checked tweed, but differs from a man's traditional flat cap, having the fashionable silhouette of a large crown contrasting with a tightly fitting band which ensured it stayed firmly on the head. A less practical example is the straw flying hat (opposite), surely susceptible to the vagaries of the wind currents swirling around the open-topped plane of the time. Happily it was more likely to have been worn by a supporter on the ground, but this would not necessarily preclude it from being swept away by the down draft of a low-flying plane. As a corrective to such incidents, the 'Breeze Hat Grip' was advertised in 1894 as 'a boone to every lady'. Available for just 3½ d, the hat grip could be fastened in one minute, and claimed to 'keep ANY SHAPE or SIZE of Ladies Hat in its position on the stormiest and windiest day'.[8]

By the 1920s more practical leather caps with chin straps were the fashion, worn by the style-conscious aviatrix. However, not all adventurers needed specialist headgear. Record-breaking pilot Lady Mary Heath felt that there was no need for helmets and goggles, preferring to fly in a simple close-fitting felt hat which allowed the go-getting girl to travel effortlessly from plane to party.[9] Motoring meanwhile, which evolved speedily as a pastime, was slow to develop suitable headgear. Women behind the wheel wore large wide-brimmed hats tied in place by a veil, essential for covering the face in a car without a windscreen. However, these were gradually replaced by wool and leather flat caps. Henry Heath of Oxford Street, originally a menswear hatter, made a name in the early decades of the twentieth century for stylish ladies' sporting hats.

Above: Table of hats, recommending the suitability of various milliners for different types of clients. From *Designing Women* by Margaretta Byers, 1930s.

Opposite page: Unknown maker/unlabelled, straw flying club hat, c.1910. The hat has a printed Petersham ribbon hatband. Jones says, 'I love this hat and the fact that the ribbon is printed with 'aero-club' but its so unsuitable for flying in!'. V&A: T.59–1936.

Below: Magazine advertisement for the 'Breeze Hat Grip', 1894.

Many iconic figures – not just fashionable women – have used hats as a way of defining their image. The simple beret – as worn by revolutionary Che Guevara (top), Johnny Rotten (see p. 18) and Faye Dunaway's glamorous gangster Bonnie in the film *Bonnie and Clyde* (opposite top) – became imbued with an edge of rebellion and danger. From the controversial Zairean president Sese Seko Mobutu's leopard-skin cap to the crown of Queen Elizabeth II, a hat confers and defines status. While the Queen wears a crown only on specific occasions, she is rarely seen in public without a hat or head covering (above right). The specifications for the design of royal hats in the twentieth century were closely tied in with the development of popular media. Hats for the Royal family had to compliment their outfit and mark them out to their subjects, while also ensuring that their faces would not be obscured from any angle. Hats worn by the young Princess Diana in the early 1980s sparked a wave of imitations (opposite bottom). The felt hat designed by John Boyd, which she wore on the evening of her wedding day, was particularly popular and replicated in all areas of the millinery market for several years to come. Ever with her finger on the pulse of British traditions and affections, Vivienne Westwood celebrated the British Royal family with her Harris Tweed crown of 1987 (right).

Opposite far left: Che Guevara, wearing his signature beret, 1960. Photograph by Alexander Korda.

Opposite left: Aage Thaarup designed this hat especially for Queen Elizabeth II to wear for Trooping the Colour, 1951.

Opposite below: Vivienne Westwood's Harris Tweed crown, 1987.

Below: Diana, Princess of Wales in a Stephen Jones hat, 1983.

Right: Faye Dunaway as Bonnie from the film *Bonnie and Clyde*, 1967.

The fashion designer as client

For many well-known milliners, collaborations with fashion houses afford them a different sort of client – the designer with whom they will work closely to create a full look or silhouette for their collection. Significantly, many of the key fashion designers of the twentieth century created their most memorable looks collaboratively with milliners, who added the all-important defining flourish for the head. Designer Paul Poiret (1879–1944) worked closely with the milliner Madeleine Panizon (active 1920s), her hats playing a vital role in completing his esoterically sumptuous creations. Twenty years later Christian Dior's collaboration with the milliner Mitza Bricard (1900–1977) helped to create some of his best-known hats. *Vogue* journalist Bettina Ballard wrote of Bricard's relationship with Dior: 'Mitza was a rare phenomenom in that she had eliminated all other interests in her life. She understood only extravagant elegance … It was she who interpreted his [Dior's] ideas for hats to complete each costume'.[10]

In 1953, London couturier Norman Hartnell (1901–79) decided to open a millinery salon in his couture house on London's Bruton Street. Hartnell approached the French milliner Claude St Cyr (1920–2002) who, recognising the benefits of being allied with the dressmaker to the Queen, agreed to extend her business to London. However, while Hartnell and St Cyr presented their designs together as ensembles, their creative processes were quite separate: 'The Bruton Street workroom was put in charge of one of the French *vendeuses*, Madame Paule, with Claude St Cyr flying regularly from Paris to supervise the production. Her Paris collection was sent over to be copied and the popularity it had at home was repeated in London'.[11] Fashion was then much more prescriptive than it is today. Seasonal silhouettes, colours and skirt lengths were internationally observed, allowing for a French collection of hats to work just as well when transported to London.

Opposite page: Mitza Bricard for Christian Dior, green silk headscarf with applied grey roses, 1969. The veil shape was a signature style for Bricard. Worn and given by Lady Abdy. V&A: T.163–1974.

Below: Hartnell coat and Claude St Cyr hat, sketched by Francis Marshall *c*.1955. V&A: Frances Marshall archive.

Norman Hartnell
hat by Claude St Cyr

Left: Stephen Jones for Comme des Garçons, autumn/winter 2007.

Opposite page: Model Christy Turlington wears a black straw and pink velvet hat by Stephen Jones for John Galliano, spring/summer 1994.

Stephen Jones follows in this lineage of designer milliner creative partnerships, working with the key designers of his generation. In the past he has worked with designers Thierry Mugler, Claude Montana and Jean-Paul Gaultier, and today his designer clients cover the globe. London-based Giles Deacon collaborates with Jones to provide the headgear for all of his shows. In New York Jones works with designer Marc Jacobs, creating collaborative hats for Jacobs' own label. Jones began designing hats for Japanese label Comme des Garçons in the 1980s, and their relationship thrives today (above). It has also inspired the development of his 'One' collection of hats for Comme des Garçons' London store, the Dover Street Market. Jones's long-standing collaboration with John Galliano has produced pieces for both Galliano's eponymous collections and his work at the houses of Givenchy and Dior.

Jones notes that working with each designer is a very different experience. In the early days of his collaboration with Comme des Garçons, before the widespread use of fax machines in the 1980s, there was no way of sending his sketches – worked from a brief – to Japan except by post, so images would take eight days to reach the designer Rei Kawakubo. While working with Thierry Mugler, Jones recalls the importance of the ability to work quickly. Mugler was very specific about what he wanted – he would sketch a hat and Jones would interpret it as closely as possible.

Above: Egyptian Anubis head, 660–300 BC. Made from layers of linen, papyrus and plaster, it was worn by a priest during funeral services.

Opposite page: Model wearing Anubis head designed by Stephen Jones for Christian Dior *haute couture*, spring 2004.

At the start of a collaboration Jones will discuss themes and inspiration with the designer, and then work up ideas and sketches and *toiles* (prototypes). These will then be tried on in the company of the designer or member of their accessories team, while a discussion takes place over what needs to be changed, from an extra topstitch to a tighter band or a higher feather. This process will continue until Jones and the collaborating designer are happy with the outcome. Some of the design houses with which Jones collaborates will make up the pieces in their own millinery workrooms, and so he will travel to these destinations to ensure that the process is all in order. At Dior *haute couture*, each hat will be tried on with each outfit (there are usually about 45 looks or outfits) and examined for changes that will need to be made. There is often a particular style of hat to go with tailored pieces and one to go with dresses. The next meeting will focus just on the hats and finalising their design details. After a series of meetings there is usually just two weeks in which the hats have to be made up and finished in time for the show. However, where Dior *haute couture* is concerned, the hats are usually dramatic statement pieces as opposed to quiet accompaniments. For the spring/summer 2004 *haute couture* show, Jones was charged with creating the giant Anubis head mask which stalked down the catwalk (opposite) and transported a mesmerised audience to a realm of fantasy that has become synonymous with Stephen Jones and John Galliano collaborations for the house of Dior.

Jones has spoken of how, for him, the process of creating a hat is akin to turning a fantasy into reality. But the fantasy mutates as everyone takes their own personal interpretation from the piece. Jones sees this as an important part of giving the object life. In such a way a good hat provides an unending source of entertainment, glamour, amusement and inspiration.

As one of the most respected milliners of his generation, Jones retains a generosity and consideration for all the milliners who work for him. For all of his experience and involvement in every aspect of his millinery production, he still believes that: 'Sometimes it is good for me not to be directly associated with the hats, because they can come out looking over-sophisticated.' After more than 25 years experience the eye becomes very refined. Sometimes someone from the workroom will pick something a little off-kilter and give the hat a freshness or a strange quirk.

This encouragement and close involvement in handing down skills is what makes millinery such a particular and unique world. The thread of experience and technique can clearly be traced back from today's young milliners to some of the more prolific millinery houses of the early twentieth century. The V&A's collaboration with Stephen Jones has revealed much of the often unrecognized, imaginative, creative and peculiar world of millinery.

Above: Selection of Stephen Jones's show invitations featuring illustrations by Robyn Neald and Julie Verhoeven.

Opposite page: Stephen Jones for Christian Dior *haute couture*, flower hat, spring 2003.

Milliners' Biographies

Adolfo
(1933–)

The American-based couturier Adolfo Sardiña served his apprenticeship in Balenciaga's hat workshop in Paris. In 1948 he emigrated to New York, where he worked as a milliner's assistant. In 1953 he became chief designer for the wholesale company Emme. In the same year, his dramatic millinery designs won a Coty Fashion Award. In 1962 he opened his own custom millinery salon, Adolfo Inc, in New York, where he began making clothes first to complement his hats, and then as his primary business. His couture clients included the Duchess of Windsor and Nancy Reagan. In 1993 he closed his salon to focus on his licensing agreements. His trademark designs include huge fur berets and small caps with visors.

Adrian, Gilbert
(Adrian Adolph Greenburg; 1903–59)

Adrian achieved lasting fame and success for his costume designs for Hollywood films in the 1920s and 1930s. Designs for stars such as Greta Garbo and Joan Crawford attracted great publicity, and were copied by the ready-to-wear industry. The accompanying hats often credited to Adrian were mostly created by Mr John of John-Frederics. In 1941 Adrian moved away from films to launch Adrian Ltd, a high-end ready-to-wear business in New York. The salon closed in 1948, though Adrian continued designing for wholesale until 1953.

Agnès
(active 1917–49)

Madame Agnès trained with Caroline Reboux, prior to opening her own salon in 1917 on the rue du Faubourg Saint-Honoré, Paris. Her hats were admired for their striking use of colour and form. She was known for cutting brims on her customer's head. During the 1920s and 1930s she was one of the most successful milliners in Paris. She retired in 1949, and died soon afterwards.

Bach, Søren
(1967–)

Søren Bach worked as a celebrity hairdresser before studying millinery at the Royal College of Art, London. For his graduate show in 2007, he applied hairdressing techniques to fur. The pelts were bleached, dyed, shaved and cut before being made into dramatic, colourful hats. His avant-garde designs won him

the Todd & Duncan Award for excellence in fashion and textile design. His creations have been worn by performers such as Björk and Grace Jones.

Fred Bare
(founded 1982)

Fred Bare Headwear was set up in 1982 by Carolyn Brooke-Davis and Anita Evagora. Their hats combine traditional British craft techniques with creative fabric treatments. These include bleaching, appliqué and various surface decoration techniques. They also operate an export side to the main business.

Barthet, Jean
(1920–2000)

Jean Barthet was one of the most prolific French milliners of the twentieth century. He occupied his showroom on the rue du Faubourg Saint-Honoré, Paris, from the 1950s for over forty years. Barthet was one of two milliners to be included as members of the Chambre Syndicale de la Couture Parisienne. In the 1960s, at the pinnacle of his career, he was referred to as *'prince de modistes'*. Barthet designed for the couture houses of Lanvin, Lagerfield and Ungaro, but also worked in film costume, making hats for films such as *A Very Private Affair* (1962) and *Chanel Solitaire* (1981). His clients included actresses Catherine Deneuve, Grace Kelly and (his close confidante) Sophia Loren, as well as pop star Michael Jackson.

Ben-Yusuf, Anna
(1845–1909)

Originally from Berlin, Anna Kind married an Algerian man who lived in London, but by 1881 she had become estranged from her husband. She emigrated to the United States in the late 1880s. By 1891 she was established in Boston as a milliner. Her daughter, Zaida Ben-Yusuf (1869–1933), also worked as a milliner in New York from about 1895, before becoming a successful portrait photographer. From 1905 to 1907 Anna Ben-Yusuf taught millinery at the Pratt Institute, New York. In 1908 she published one of the first reference books on millinery technique.

Bernstock Speirs
(founded 1982)

Paul Bernstock and Thelma Speirs studied fashion together at Middlesex University. In 1982 they established their label, Bernstock Speirs. They made

trend-led hats for day-to-day wear, rather than for special occasions. Their designs, inspired by the underground club and music scene, sell on a global scale. Producing young and sporty seasonal hat collections for men and women, their work combines traditional hat-making techniques with unusual fabrics, colours and ideas. In 2004 they opened their first dedicated shop in Shoreditch, London, where customers can view the designers at work in their studio.

Bes-Ben
(active 1920s to '50s)

In 1920 Benjamin Green-Field (1897–1989) opened his first Bes-Ben hatshop in Chicago. The hats were so popular that by 1930 four additional shops were opened to supply demand. In 1941 Benjamin Green-Field created his first 'silly' hat – a design trimmed with miniature Dalmatian dogs. The whimsical 'silly' hats with their unexpected trimmings (including doll furniture, razors and chessmen) earned him the title of 'Chicago's Mad Hatter' through the 1940s and 1950s.

Bertin, Rose
(1747–1813)

In 1772, Marie-Jeanne 'Rose' Bertin opened an aristocratic dressmaking and millinery establishment in the rue du Faubourg Saint-Honoré, Paris. In 1774 she was introduced to her best-known customer, Marie Antoinette, Queen of France. With the Queen as customer, Rose Bertin became so widely known that she is considered the first celebrity fashion designer. European aristocracy and royalty came to her for gowns, caps and headdresses that reflected the extravagance of pre-Revolutionary Parisian fashion. She survived the French Revolution of 1789–95 relatively unscathed, though her business never recovered.

Boyd, John
(1925–)

Since establishing his millinery business in 1946, John Boyd has been recognised as one of London's most respected milliners. He entered the millinery trade through an apprenticeship with Aage Thaarup. His millinery salon is located on London's exclusive Beauchamp Place, and his clients include members of the Royal family. The tricorne which he designed for Princess Diana's going-away outfit inspired thousands of copies throughout the 1980s.

The Milliner's Costume, engraving by Bonnart, Musée Carnavelet

Habit de Chapellier

Bricard, Mitza
(Germaine Bricard; 1900–1977)
Mitza Bricard was a close friend and muse to the couturier Christian Dior. She was notorious for her mysterious origins and her exotic style, featuring leopard spots and extravagant jewellery. When Dior launched in 1947, she advised on the accessories for his outfits. In 1948 she took charge of Dior's millinery department, where she supervised output through the 1950s and 1960s. Under Bricard, Dior hats often combined neat forms with unusual profiles and boldly extravagant decoration.

Chanel, Coco
(Gabrielle Chanel; 1883–1971)
In 1908 Chanel launched a millinery business from the Paris apartment of Etienne Balsan, with whom she was romantically involved. In 1910, with the backing of 'Boy' Capel, she moved to commercial premises at 21 rue Cambon, Paris. Providing hats to leading Parisian actresses of the day, she worked exclusively as a milliner until 1913, when she sold her first garments. In 1916 she presented her first *couture* collection, where simple wide-brimmed hats complemented relaxed jersey ensembles. By the 1920s the House of Chanel had gained an enduring reputation as one of the great Paris fashion houses of the twentieth century.

Daché, Lilly
(1898–1989)
Lilly Daché was born in France and apprenticed with the Paris milliners Mme Georgette, Suzanne Talbot and Caroline Reboux. In 1924 she emmigrated to the United States, where she quickly made a name for herself with her dramatic custom millinery. In addition to her millinery business, she designed headwear for Hollywood costume designer Travis Banton. The actress Carmen Miranda's famous towering flower-bedecked turbans were Daché creations. In the 1950s Lilly Daché launched two ready-to-wear hat lines, 'Mme Lilly' and 'Dachette's'. She retired in 1968.

Denford, Nigel & Carol
(active 1982–)
Nigel and Carol Denford founded The Hat Shop in Neal Street, Covent Garden, London, in 1982. They sold both male and female headwear, and their business succeeded at a time when the hat trade in general was not doing well. In 1999, however, they closed down due to rising costs. They then founded the successful trade journal *The Hat Magazine*, which has global circulation.

Fox, Frederick
(1931–)
Australian-born milliner Frederick Fox learnt his trade at Sydney hatters J.L. Normoyle. In 1958 he moved to London to work with Otto Lucas and Mitzi Lorenz, before taking over the hat firm Langee and opening his own millinery salon in London's Brook Street in 1964. A great favourite of the Royal family, he was one of the Queen's most long-standing millinery designers. He retired from millinery in 2002 and returned to Australia, where he is a patron of the Australian Millinery Association.

Gordon, Jo
(1968–)
Scottish designer Jo Gordon combines modern techniques with traditional materials from her home country. From her London studio she creates one-off pieces for exhibitions and magazines, whilst more commercial designs for export are made in Scotland. Her interest in sustainability issues means that the Scottish workshop uses local materials. Gordon also uses recycled packaging to minimise her company's carbon footprint.

Halston
(Roy Halston Frowick; 1932–90)
In 1953, while working as a window dresser in Chicago, Halston was invited by hairdresser André Basil to set up his own millinery atelier in the latter's hairdressing salon, based at the city's fashionable Ambassador Hotel. The success of this venture led to a job offer in 1958 from New York's leading milliner Lilly Daché, where Halston worked as designer and manager of her wholesale hat division. In 1959 he joined the New York department store Bergdorf-Goodman, where he became the first in-house milliner to design under his own name. His purist, minimalist designs, which included Jackie Kennedy's pillbox hats, were very successful. In 1966 Bergdorf-Goodman allowed him to launch a ready-to-wear clothing range, and two years later Halston moved away from millinery to launch his fashion label.

Harada, Misa
(1968–)
Misa Harada is a Japanese designer based in London. After graduating from the Royal College of Art, London, in 1994 she worked as a designer for Frederick Fox until 1998, when she opened her own business. Her designs are popular with celebrities, both for performance and wearing in the street. Her signature style is based upon classic forms, unexpected colours and strongly textured materials trimmed with leather or metal.

Henry Heath
(active 1822–1960s)
The hatter Henry Heath founded his company in 1822 in Holborn, London and it continued trading for over a hundred years. In 1839 he moved his business to Oxford Street, where he made a name for himself manufacturing gentlemen's silk top hats. As time went by Henry Heath also supplied bowler hats and other gentlemen's headwear. Despite the prestige of providing hats to the Royal family, the business closed in the 1960s.

House of Flora
(Flora McLean; b.1971)
This label was established by Flora McLean, a graduate of the Royal College of Art, London, where she was taught by Shirley Hex. House of Flora is noted for its sculptural and architecturally inspired hats, made from technologically innovative materials such as latex, PVC and Perspex. In collaboration with Neil Moodie, McLean also produces a collection of 'Hairts' – hats based on iconic hair-styles.

John Frederics
(active 1928–48)
Founded in 1928 by Frederic Hirst and the mysterious John Harburger (or Harberger), their first salon was in a small apartment over Delman's shoe store in Madison Avenue, New York. The business swiftly prospered, expanding into elite branches in Palm Beach, Miami and Hollywood, and outlets in seven hundred major department stores. In 1940 the label earned sixty million dollars in the American market alone. John-Frederics hats featured in many Hollywood films, most famously *Gone With The Wind* (1939). In 1948 the business was disbanded. Frederic Hirst continued under the label 'Mr Fred', while John became John P. John, or Mr John.

Mr John
(c.1904–93)
Little is known for certain about the origins of this flamboyant New York milliner. He assumed this name in 1948, following the dissolving of his John-Frederics partnership with Frederic Hirst. The 'Mr John' six-storey salon opened in 57th Street, New York, in 1948, where it remained until its closure in 1970. Having started out with ten employees, by the 1950s he was employing two hundred and fifty, while his annual turnover averaged at seven million dollars (a fifth of this from custom hats alone). He is credited with popularising wimples, crocheted hats and scarf hats. His designs could be fantastic, or extremely understated. His hats were made for any and every occasion, from balls to advertisements. He was renowned for the film hats he made whilst at John-Frederics, and continued to do so under his own name, creating hats for films such as *My Fair Lady* (1963) and *Death in Venice* (1971). After his business closed in 1970, he continued to make hats for private clients until his death.

Kokin
(1959–)
Kokin trained at the Fashion Institute of Technology, undertaking night classes. Since his debut in 1984, Kokin has worked with fashion designers including Bill Blass, Oscar de la Renta, Pauline Trigère and Giorgio Sant' Angelo. In 1991 and 1992 Kokin was awarded the Millinery Designer of the Year, and again in 1994. He launched his ready-to-wear range in 1996. In 2000 he designed hats for the Robert Altman film, *Dr T and The Women*, in which actresses Liv Tyler and Kate Hudson wore his creations. His clients have included Grace Jones, Julia Roberts, Britney Spears, Alicia Keys, Sharon Stone and First Lady, Laura Bush.

Lanvin, Jeanne
(1867–1946)
In 1885, the 18-year old Jeanne Lanvin opened her first small millinery workshop in Paris. Four years later she opened a millinery house in the rue Boissy-d'Anglas, Paris. Her hats showed a keen eye for colour and form, but it was the dresses made for her daughter Marguerite (1897–1958) that captured her clientele's attention. Between 1908 and 1909 Lanvin developed her dressmaking business, selling

children's and women's fashions and becoming a couturier. Until her death, Lanvin continued designing hats to complement her clothes. The House of Lanvin remains in business, selling clothing, accessories and perfumes.

LeRoy, Louis-Hippolyte
(1763–1829)
Louis-Hippolyte LeRoy started out as a hairdresser in pre-Revolutionary Paris. After the Revolution, he became a dressmaker and milliner. He dressed nobility and royalty across Europe and Russia, his most famous client being Napoleon Bonaparte's first wife, Josephine. His hats were highly regarded, with *toques* a particular speciality. Among his innovations were *chapeaux de paille* (straw hats trimmed with feathers in the same colour), and the use of double-faced satin ribbon. He was based at the Maison Boutin, rue de Richelieu, Paris, from 1802 until his retirement in 1821.

List, Adele
(1893–1983)
Viennese milliner, Adele List rejected traditional hat-making rules to experiment with her own techniques. She disregarded applied trimmings and decorations, choosing instead to mould her materials into dramatic sculptural shapes. Her hats were one-off pieces or made in a limited series by a small team of milliners in her Vienna atelier. A show of her hats in Berlin in 1937 attracted much attention and List was sought by top German fashion houses to make their hats. However her main collaboration was with couturièr Gertrud Hochsmann. List worked independently of fashion trends and felt the key element in hat design was relating the hat to the customer.

Lola
(1946–)
Dutch-born but raised in France, Lola Ehrlich moved to New York after being widowed. She worked for a craft magazine and undertook evening hatmaking classes at the Fashion Institute of Technology. In December 1989 she established her eponymous label in a small shop-front in the East Village. Her ateliers are now based in the Garment District. She has collaborated with New York designers including Ralph Lauren, Donna Karan, Michael Kors and accessories designer

Kate Spade. Lola has also worked with Earl Jeans, Nike and The Gap.

Lucile
(Lady Lucy Christiana Duff Gordon; 1862–1935)
The fashion house of Lucile was founded in 1889, quickly establishing a reputation for romanticism, lavish trimming and attention to detail. Lucile made both fashionable clothing and theatrical costumes, most notably for the operetta *The Merry Widow* (1907). The extravagantly large, flower-laden hats she made for this production proved popular with her customers. Lucile also designed simpler hats, often featuring unusual colour combinations and dramatic trimming. Her fashion house had salons in New York, Chicago and Paris, as well as in London. After leaving Lucile Ltd in about 1922, Lucile worked on an individual basis with private clients. Her autobiography, *Discretions and Indiscretions*, was published in 1932.

Malyard
(in business 1954–85)
Malyard was one of London's leading hatters and milliners, supplying both wholesale and retail customers. They made both male and female hats. George Mallard founded the company in 1954, trading under his own name until about 1966. The company became Malyard Hats, and later just Malyard. Originally based on Ganton Street, London, the company relocated to Kingly Street in 1970 and finally to Lavender Hill. George Mallard stopped designing in 1981, and retired in 1985 when the company ceased trading.

Marie Mercie
(1942–)
In 1987, following a career in journalism and plastic surgery, Marie Mercie turned to making hats. She met Anthony Peto (now an internationally recognised milliner) and together they opened their first shop in Paris. Mercie then established her own boutique on Saint-Sulpice, where she has been based ever since. Every season she organises small exhibitions in her shop, which sells ready-to wear range, a couture line and offers a bespoke bridal service. In 2001 she opened two boutiques in London and her hats are sold in Europe, the United States and Japan. She is the author of *Voyages autour d'un chapeau* (1990) and *Chapeaux Secrets* (2003).

Mirman, Simone
(1912–2008)
Trained with the prolific milliner Rose Valois, Mirman began her career designing hats for Elsa Schiaparelli. She moved to London in 1937 where she took over the running of Schiaparelli's hat department. Two years later she set up her own business which flourished for the next 30 years. Mirman was resolute about suiting the right hat to the right woman. Her designs had a playfulness of touch but were always relevant and wearable. She created hats for Christian Dior and Norman Hartnell and her clients included Princess Margaret, the Queen and the Queen Mother. She retired in 1990 and returned to France to paint.

Panizon, Madeleine
(active 1920s)
Madeleine Panizon studied at Paul Poiret's art school, the École Martine. The school encouraged young women to design in total creative freedom. Their designs were developed into textiles for fashion and furnishings. Poiret kept an eye on the students, and noted Madeleine Panizon's talent for millinery. After the École Martine closed in 1919, he commissioned her to make hats to complement his graphic, exotic fashions during the 1920s.

Paulette
(Mme de la Bruyère; 1900–84)
The 'Paulette Modes' salon was opened in 1939 on the avenue Franklin D. Roosevelt, Paris. Paulette became famous for her draped woollen turbans during the Second World War. After the war, she designed and made hats for top couturier Robert Piguet. In addition to her turbans, she was also known for small caps entirely covered in feathers. Her hats were known for their lightness. Up until her death in 1984, she designed hats for many fashion designers, including Pierre Cardin, Thierry Mugler and Coco Chanel.

Prudence
(active 1990–)
A regular of New York's Fashion Institute of Technology, Prudence left New York and moved to London in 1986 where she trained to be a milliner. She launched her own label 'Prudence' in 1990, and in the same year began an ongoing collaboration with Vivienne Westwood. She has worked with Balenciaga, Gucci, London

hatters Herbert Johnson, and Tom Ford at Yves Saint Laurent. She currently creates hats for designers Charles Anastase and Julien McDonald. Prudence has taught millinery in Germany, America and Japan. Along with her collaborative partnerships she designs her own line of knitwear hats sold exclusively in Japan.

Rebaté, Lucienne
(dates)
Lucienne Rebaté was employed by Chanel, before joining Caroline Reboux in the early 1920s. She became director of Caroline Reboux in 1927 following the founder's death, and ensured its continued success throughout the 1930s. Reboux designs during this period include the lace halo hat with wreath that Wallis Simpson wore to marry the Duke of Windsor.

Reboux, Caroline
(1837–1927)
In the mid-nineteenth century Caroline Reboux's hats caught the attention of Princess Metternich, who also 'discovered' the couturier Charles Frederick Worth. It was through the Princess's patronage that Reboux became milliner to the Empress Eugenie. In 1870 she opened an aristocratic millinery establishment at 23 rue de la Paix, Paris. The reputation of Caroline Reboux as one of Paris's finest milliners lasted up to and beyond her death in 1927. Under the direction of Lucienne Rebaté, Caroline Reboux hats remained in demand throughout the 1930s. The establishment eventually closed in 1956.

Rees, Dai
(1961–)
Dai Rees, who studied at St Martin's Royal College of Art, London, launched his millinery business in 1997. He was known for his spectacular headdresses and sculptural hats, and also produced several womenswear collections. In 2002 he closed his fashion label, and is currently working as an artist-cum-researcher, examining fine handicraft techniques and the role of the maker.

Reslaw Hats/Paul Walser Ltd
(active 1906–c.1980)
Reslaw Hats was founded in 1906 from a Swiss straw-plait and braid business. Their factory was based in Luton, England, where there was a thriving hat industry. Until its closure in about 1980, Reslaw was one of the main suppliers of

fur felts and straws to the high-end millinery trade.

Rudolf
(1913–1980)
Rudolf was a milliner of high repute in Prague. In 1948, upon visiting London at the time of the coup d'état in Czechoslavakia (now the Czech Republic), Rudolf chose and was granted permission to reside in England. He soon became known as a foremost milliner. He designed for royalty, notably Queen Elizabeth, the Queen Mother until the time of his death. He drew his clients from the theatre, English society and London couturiers, with whom he collaborated throughout his career.

Schiaparelli, Elsa
(1890–1973)
Elsa Schiaparelli opened her fashion house in Paris in 1928. While she is famed for her outrageous fashion designs, their accompanying accessories and hats were equally important to her. She designed a huge variety of hats, using all kinds of materials and sources of inspiration. Her surrealist designs, including the 1937 'Shoe Hat', were particularly notorious. Schiaparelli closed her couture house in 1954. Due to a licensing deal struck with American manufacturers in 1949, Schiaparelli hats, lingerie and accessories remained available in American department stores until her death.

Shilling, David
(1956–)
David Shilling first became interested in hats at the age of 12, when he began to assist his mother Gertrude Shilling in designing her notorious Ascot hats. He worked as an Underwriter at Lloyds of London before opening his own model millinery store in London's Marylebone High Street in 1976. His work was stocked in New York by the department stores Bloomingdales and Bergdorf Goodman. In contrast to his flamboyant couture hats he launched a ready-to-wear collection in 1984. Having relocated to Monaco, Shilling now focuses on art and design consultancy.

Smith, Graham
(1938–)
A graduate of the Royal College of Art, Smith worked with the Parisian couture house of Lanvin Castillo while still a student.

On his return to London he designed hats for Michael of Carlos Place. In 1967 he set up his own business and became one of London's most noted milliners, recognised for his technical skill and the lightness of his creations. He designed headgear for fashion designers Zandra Rhodes and Jean Muir. Since closing his business in 1981, he has worked as a millinery consultant for companies such as Kangol and BHS.

Smith, Justin
(1978–)
Justin Smith showed his first millinery collection at London Fashion Week in February 2008. He originally trained as a hairdresser, having launched in 2000 a successful London hairdressing salon called 'And People Like Us'. At the same time he began training as a milliner. He studied at Kensington & Chelsea College, and did an MA in Millinery at the Royal College of Art, London. His graduate show was a great success, attracting much attention. His labels are 'J. Smith Esquire' and 'Mister Smith'.

Somerville, Philip
(1930–)
Philip Somerville established his business in 1972 as a wholesale milliner supplying London department stores, including Harrods, Harvey Nichols, Fenwicks, Fortnum and Mason and Selfridges. The business was also successful in the American market and hats were distributed to Bergdorf Goodman, Saks 5th Avenue and Neiman Marcus. In 1987, the Somerville hat salon opened in Bond Street for private clients. The Queen and Diana, Princess of Wales were regular clients, and Somerville was awarded the Royal Warrant: Milliner to the Queen in 1995. Today, Somerville continues to create headwear for the Queen, as well as producing a range of ready-to-wear and couture hats.

St. Cyr, Claude
(Simone Naudet, 1920–2002)
French milliner Claude St. Cyr trained in London, and worked in Paris in the 1930s and 1940s, before opening a London workshop in about 1950. She closed her doors in 1972. Her understated, perfectly proportioned hats were a great success with her clientele, which included members of the Royal Family. She worked closely with Princess (later Queen) Elizabeth,

even supplying a padded velvet cap for the 1953 Coronation to help support the Crown of St Edward.

Stewart, Noel
(1978–)
Noel Stewart trained with Dai Rees (1999) and Stephen Jones (2000-02) before doing an MA in Millinery at the Royal College of Art, London. After graduation he designed for Phillip Somerville, while launching his own label for autumn/winter 2003. He has provided hats for several designers' shows, including Roland Mouret and Paul Costelloe. His commercial collections are stocked by the department stores Barneys, New York and Selfridges, London. His sculptural designs either make dramatic statements, or are elegantly understated and wearable.

Suzy, Madame
(active 1920s–'50s)
Based at 5, rue de la Paix, Paris, Madame Suzy's designs first rose to prominence in the 1920s. She popularised the turban in the late 1930s, a style which became incredibly popular during the war as it could be easily appropriated under shortages. In 1941, American department store Bergdorf Goodman devoted a section to Suzy's hats. With Paris under occupation, French fashion production was limited but Suzy continued to receive orders from the United States. She continued to design hats into the 1950s, and her clients include *American Harper's Bazaar*.

Svend
(active 1950s–60s)
Svend was a Danish milliner who came to Paris to work for the couturier Jacques Fath. His millinery salon opened in the 1950s at 50, rue Ponthieu. Fath hats were often dramatic, using striking materials such as fur, both real and faux, and printed dress cottons. Svend also designed for the couturiers Jacques Heim and Jacques Griffe.

Talbot, Suzanne
(active 1900s–1950s)
The millinery house of Suzanne Talbot opened in 1907 at 10-14 rue Royale, Paris, later relocating to 8 avenue Matignon. She was particularly popular in the 1920s and 1930s for her dramatic yet restrained hats. The salon also offered accessories to co-ordinate with its hats, such as gloves and parasols. Several milliners,

including Paulette and Lilly Daché, were apprenticed with Suzanne Talbot. She died during the Second World War, though the establishment continued under the direction of one of her milliners until its closure in 1956.

Thaarup, Aage
(1906–87)
Danish born Aage Thaarup spent the early years of his career between Berlin, Paris, London and India. In 1932 he returned to London, where he set up a millinery salon in fashionable Berkeley Square. Although he was not a trained milliner and never learnt to sew, his charm and vision made his business a popular destination for women of fashion. He made hats for the Queen, the Queen Mother and Princess Margaret, and in the post-war period launched his more affordable 'Teen and Twenty' range. His autobiography *Heads and Tales* was published in 1956.

Treacy, Philip
(1967–)
As a fashion student, Irish-born milliner Philip Treacy studied at the National College of Art and Design in Dublin, then interned with Stephen Jones before specialising in millinery design at the Royal College of Art. Taught by Shirley Hex, Treacy developed an impeccable technique and received great acclaim on graduating in 1990. His work was championed from early on by the fashion stylist Isabella Blow. Spearheading hat fashions in the 1990s, he worked extensively with feathers, fashioning them into incredible and unusual shapes. He has worked on diffusion lines with Debenhams department store and has collaborated with designers such as Karl Lagerfeld at Chanel, Rifat Ozbek, Valentino and Ralph Lauren.

Underwood, Patricia
(1947–)
British-born milliner Patricia Underwood has resided in New York since 1967. Five years after her transatlantic move, she undertook an evening class in hat-making at the Fashion Institute of Technology. She worked with Lipp Holmfeld, manufacturing hats for two years, prior to launching her own brand in 1976. Her awards include the Coty American Fashion Critics award (1982), a Council of Fashion Design in America award (1983) and the American Accessories Achievement Award

(1992). She has worked with prominent American fashion designers, including Bill Blass, Oscar de la Renta, Ralph Lauren, Marc Jacobs and Jill Stuart.

Valois, Rose
(active 1927–70)
Rose Valois was a Parisian milliner based at 18 rue Royale from 1927 to her retirement in 1970. She trained with Caroline Reboux. An artist as well as a milliner, she applied her painterly eye for colour to her hats. She was noted for the originality and good quality of her designs.

Vernier, Madame Rose
(active 1960s)
Vernier was a French milliner who worked in Britain designing hats for fashion couturiers, including Hardy Amies, Charles Creed, Digby Morton and (the Swiss, but British-based fashion designer) Giuseppe Mattli. In 1967 she established the Franka-Vernier label with the Yugoslavian Baroness Stael von Holstein, a designer in *haute couture* garments for royalty and high society. Vernier opened her own premises on London's Dover Street in 1968. Her clients included ballerina Dame Margot Fonteyn.

Victor, Sally
(1905–77)
Sally Victor learned about millinery from the customer's point of view. Between 1923 and 1927 she worked as a buyer for the department stores Macy's, New York, and Bamberger's, New Jersey. She married the New York milliner 'Serge' (Sergiu Victor) in 1927, becoming a designer for his salon. In 1934 she opened her own custom millinery salon on 53rd Street, New York. Her hats were always sophisticated and wearable. She was inspired by painters such as Van Gogh and Mondrian, and also cited architecture as an influence. Her ready-to-wear line, 'Sally V', was launched in 1951. She retired and closed her salon in 1968.

Wedge, James
(1939–)
James Wedge trained at Walthamstow Art School and the Royal College of Art, London, specialising in millinery. He was signed up as house milliner to the London couturier Ronald Paterson, where his extreme designs attracted publicity. The department store Liberty's then offered him a free workshop in exchange for first choice of his hats. In 1962, James Wedge set up a millinery establishment in Ganton Street, London. He went on to co-own two boutiques, 'Countdown' and 'Top Gear' on King's Road, London, during the late 1960s. After Countdown closed in 1971, he became a fashion photographer and, more recently, a painter.

Woodward, Kirsten
(1961–)
Kirsten Woodward originally sold her hats through Hyper Hyper, the 1980s–1990s London store for up-and-coming 'alternative' and avant-garde designers. Her surreal designs drew the attention of the couturier Karl Lagerfeld, who commissioned her hats for his mid-80s catwalk shows at Chanel. This exposure won her huge international acclaim and recognition.

Woolland Bros
(active 1869–1967)
Woolland Brothers opened in 1869 as a modest draper's at No. 2, Lowndes Terrace, London. By 1892 it had expanded into a large department store, with a high class clientele. In the early twentieth century their millinery department was particularly smart, boasting a selection of specially imported Paris hats. The original milliners, including Suzanne Talbot, often had their labels replaced by Woollands' own. Bought by Debenhams in 1949, the Woollands site was sold for redevelopment in 1967. The Sheraton Park Tower Hotel now stands on the site.

Notes

Introduction

1. Ethyle Campbell, *Can I Help You Madam?* (London, 1938)
2. *Etcetera* magazine, May 16–29 1985, pp.26–29

Inspiration

1. Stephen Jones interview with Oriole Cullen, V&A, November 2007
2. 'Suzanne Talbot's Invention', *New York Times*, 15 March 1914
3. Edward T. James, *Notable American Women 1607–1940* (Harvard University Press, 1990)
4. Benjamin B. Green-Field Foundation: www.greenfieldfoundation.org (website consulted on 2.2.08)
5. Aage Thaarup, *Heads and Tales* (London, 1956), p.123
6. Cecil Beaton, *Fashion: An Anthology by Cecil Beaton* (London, 1971)

Creation

1. Lesley Robeson in conversation with Oriole Cullen at Stephen Jones Millinery, 25 April 2008 and 30 May 2008
2. Stephen Jones in conversation with Oriole Cullen, November 2007
3. Craig West interviewed at Stephen Jones Millinery, 22 July 2008.
4. Deborah Miller interviewed at Stephen Jones Millinery, 25 April 2008
5. Ibid.
6. *Queen*, London, April 1893
7. *New York Times*, 25 February 1910
8. Apprenticeship and Skilled Employment Association of London. Report from 1914
9. James Wedge interviewed at the V&A in February 2006
10. Deborah Miller interviewed at Stephen Jones Millinery, 25 April 2008
11. Suzy Menkes, *International Herald Tribune*, London 5 March 1996
12. Stephen Jones in conversation with Oriole Cullen at Stephen Jones Millinery, 14 June 2008
13. Stephen Jones in conversation with Oriole Cullen at Museum of London, August 2007

The Salon

1. Christopher Grey, 'Streetscapes', *New York Times*, 2 May 2004
2. Bianca M. du Mortier, *Chapeau, Chapeaux! Hats 1650–1960* (Amsterdam, 1997)
3. 'Suzanne Talbot's Invention', *New York Times*, 15 March 1914
4. C.W. Forester, *Success Through Dress* (London 1925), p.48
5. Woman's Institute of Domestic Arts and Sciences, *Harmony In Dress* (London, undated but from the 1930s), p.94
6. Lilly Daché, *Talking Through My Hats* (New York, 1946), p.6
7. Barbara Hulanicki, *From A to Biba* (London 1983), p.116
8. The Hat Shop press release, spring/summer 1996
9. Jean Rhys, *Good Morning, Midnight* (London, 1939), p.58
10. Aage Thaarup, *Heads and Tales* (London, 1956), p.215

The Client

1. Tamsin Blanchard, 'Rebel de Jour', *Observer Magazine*, 15 August 2004
2. Annie Taylor, *Guardian*, 7 March 1996
3. Meriel McCooey, *Sunday Times Magazine*, June 1977
4. Brigid Keenan, *The Women We Wanted to Look Like* (London, 1977), p.53
5. Alison Adburgham, 'Our Hats', *Punch*, 23 May 1956
6. Woman's Institute of Domestic Arts and Sciences, *Harmony In Dress* (London, n.d,) p.92
7. Stephen Jones, November 2007
8. *Queen*, London, 1894
9. Lindie Naughton, *Lady Icarus* (Dublin, 2004), pp.89–90
10. Bettina Ballard, *In My Fashion* (New York 1960), pp.229, 238
11. Poppy Richard *Everybody's Weekly*, 25 September 1954, p.34

Further Reading

Amphlett, Hilda *Hats: A History of Fashion In Headwear*, Buckinghamshire, 1974
Beaton, Cecil and Ginsburg, Madeleine *Fashion: An Anthology by Cecil Beaton*, 1971
Bendavid-Val, Leah *National Geographic Moments: Hats*, 2004
Ben-Yusuf, Mme Anna *The Art of Millinery*, 1909
Brand, Jan and Teunissen, Jose (eds) *Fashion and Accessories*, Arnhem, 2007
Clark, Fiona *Hats*, London, 1982
Crafts Council *Satellites of Fashion*, London, 1998
Crill, Rosemary *Hats from India*, London, 1985
Daché, Lilly *Talking Through My Hats*, London, 1946
De La Haye, Amy (ed.) *The Cutting Edge: 50 Years of British Fashion 1947–1997*, London, 1997
Hempstead, Laurene *Colour and Line in Dress*, New York, 1931
Henschel, Georgie *The Well Dressed Woman*, London, 1951
Hopkins, Susie *The Century of Hats*, London, 1999
Hughes, Claire *Dressed in Fiction*, Oxford, 2006
Lapidus, Olivier *La Mémoire du Geste*, Paris, 2003
MacKenzie, Althea *Hats and Bonnets*, London, 2004
McDowell, Colin *Hats: Status, Style and Glamour*, London, 1992
Poiret, Paul *King of Fashion: The Autobiography of Paul Poiret*, London 2009
Reed, Paula and Etherington-Smith, Meredith *Philip Treacy*, 2001
Reynolds, Helen *A Fashionable History Of Hats and Hairstyles*, 2004
Richter, Mme Eva *The ABC of Millinery*, London, 1950
Treacy, Philip *When Philip Met Isabella*, 2002

Museum Collections

UK
Victoria and Albert Museum, London, England
Museum of London, London, England
Hat Works, the Museum of Hatting, Stockport, England
Luton Museum and Art Gallery, Luton, England
Fashion Museum, Bath, England
Snowshill Manor, Snowshill, Gloucestershire, England
National Museum of Costume, Dumfriesshire, Scotland
Ulster Museum, Belfast, Northern Ireland

Europe
Musée de la Mode et du Textile, Louvre, Paris, France
Musée de la Mode et du Costume, Palais Galliera, Paris, France
Atelier-musée du chapeau, Chazelles-sur-Lyon, France
Galleria del Costume, Palazzo Pitti, Florence, Italy
Modemuseum in Stadt Museum, Munich, Germany
Mode Museum, Vienna, Austria
Museo del Traje, Madrid, Spain
Mode Museum, Antwerp, Belgium

North America
Costume Institute at the Metropolitan Museum of Art, New York, US
The Museum at the Fashion Institute of Technology, New York, US
Los Angeles County Museum of Art, Los Angeles, US
Philadelphia Museum of Art, Philadelphia, US
Chicago History Museum, Chicago, US
Royal Ontario Museum, Toronto, Canada

Japan
Costume Museum, Kyoto, Japan

Acknowledgements

This book is the result of the efforts and expertise of a wide range of generous contributors. Foremost I would like to thank Stephen Jones for allowing me the pleasure of his company while working on this project for over two years. I would also like to thank all at Stephen Jones Millinery; Lesley Robeson, Alexis Teplin, Cornelia De Uphaugh, Leila Abu El Hawa, Craig West, Deborah Miller and all in the salon and the workroom, and thanks to Adel Rootstein for generously lending mannequins. I would also like to express my gratitude to all of the lenders to the exhibition for their generous contributions.

I would like to thank Claire Wilcox and Betty Jackson for championing this project from the early stages. I am indebted to all of my colleagues at the V&A's Furniture Textiles and Fashion, Contemporary and Research Departments. Many thanks are due to Lesley Miller, Edwina Ehrman, Liz Miller and Christopher Breward for their support and helpful comments. Thank you to Daniel Milford-Cottam for his time and contributions to the milliner's biographies and to Sonnet Stanfill and Gareth Williams for their unflagging support and good humour. A special thanks is due to the wonderful volunteers who assisted on the project; Carly Eck, Keren Protheroe, Beth Robinson, Samantha Safer and Gemma Williams. I would also like to acknowledge the support of Anjali Bulley and Laura Potter in V&A Publishing and I am indebted to Richard Davis for his patience and expertise in photographing Stephen Jones' studio and the V&A hat collection.

Thank you to Lawrence Mynott, for his wonderful illustrations, to editor Miranda Harrison and to designers Lisa Sjukur and Damian Schober at Co Studio Design. Many thanks are due to Madeleine Ginsburg for her generosity in sharing her knowledge and recollections of the Beaton exhibiton. I am grateful to Dr Timothy Morley for his time, comments and suggestions and to Laurie Britton Newell for keeping all in order. To all at Knockaderry, thank you for the matchless support and encouragement.

Picture Credits

Images and copyright clearance have been kindly supplied as listed below (in alphabetical order by institution or surname). Unless otherwise stated, images are © V&A Images.

85, 111
© ADAGP, Paris and
DACS, London 2008

28
Les Arts Decoratifs,
Paris. Photo: Laurent
Sully Jaulmes. Tout
droits reserves.

109
© Robin Anderson /
Rex Features

81
Photography © The Art
Institute of Chicago

19, 33, 34, 35, 47, 71,
78, 105
© Peter Ashworth, www.
ashworth-photos.com

42, 49
Courtesy of BFI

9
© BnF / Photo:
Seeberger, October 1927

25, 82
René Bouché / Vogue
© The Condé Nast
Publications Ltd.

118
The Bridgeman
Art Library

65
© Buhrle Collection,
Zurich, Switzerland /
The Bridgeman Art
Library

24, 52, 62
Courtesy of Christian
Dior Couture © Rights
Reserved

66
© Collection, Archives
Charmet / The
Bridgeman Art Library

13
© Alessandro Dal
Bruoni

31
Fabrizio Ferri / Vogue
© The Condé Nast
Publications Ltd.

13, 48, 86, 88, 98, 99, 108
Courtesy of, and ©
Getty Images

115
© Harrogate Museums
and Art Gallery, North
Yorkshire, UK / The
Bridgeman Art Library

84
© Harrods Archive

11
© Hulton-Deutsch
Collection / CORBIS

93
© Imperial War
Museum, H 4367

14
Courtesy of, and ©
Herb Ritts Foundation.
Originally published in
The New Yorker

93
© Imperial War
Museum, H 4367

72
Courtesy of JSmith
Esquire

23
© www.
justinephotography.com

108
© Nick Knight

89
Photo: Kirby Koh for
Stephen Jones at Dover
Street Market

108
Alexander Korda

14
© Charles & Josette
Lenars / CORBIS

20
© Mike Maloney / Rex
Features

68, 87
© Photo by Leonard
Mccombe / Time & Life
Pictures / Getty Images

29
© Steven Meisel

12
© 1957 Metro-Goldwyn-
Mayer Studios Inc. All
Rights Reserved

103
© Yui Mok/PA Wire

54
© Chris Moore, 2002

113
© Chris Moore, 2003

114
© Chris Moore, 2004
63, 93
© Chris Moore, 2007

72
© Chris Moore, 2008

43
Courtesy of MovieStore
Collection

79
© Museum Folkwang
Essen

71, 78
© Museum of London

Front cover, title page,
26, 50, 76, 94
Lawrence Myott

38
Photo: Laetitia Negre

90
© Ormond Gigli

97
© Miguel Reveriego /
CLM UK

102
© Tim Rooke / Rex
Features

101, 109
© Rex Features

16
© John Slater /
CORBIS

18
© Ray Stevenson /
Rex Features

17
Courtesy of the Royal
Liverpool Philharmonic

6, 11, 16, 21, 22, 32, 34,
35, 39, 41, 46, 47, 55, 56,
70, 112, 116, 117
Courtesy of Stephen
Jones Millinery

15, 98
© Time & Life Pictures /
Getty Images

80-81
© Marianne Topham,
Courtesy of the Museum
of London
21
Courtesy of Yohji
Yamamoto Press
© Monica Feudi

30
© Richard Young /
Rex Features

Index

Figures in *italics* refer to illustrations and captions

Adburgham, Alison 102
Adolfo (Adolfo Sardiña)
  16, 118
Adrian, Gilbert (Adrian
  Greenburg) 118
  hats *43*
Agnès, Madame 31, *31*, 87,
  87, 118
  millinery salon 87
Amies, Hardy 122
  ensemble *18*
Anastase, Charles 120
Ashley, Iris *84*
Attainville, Vladzio d' 23

Bach, Søren 72, 118
  fur hat *103*
Balenciaga 18, 20, 23, 99,
  118, 120
  straw beret 36, *36*
Ballard, Bettina 111
Ballets Russes 92
Balsan, Etienne 119
Banton, Travis 119
Bare, Fred 88, 118
Barthet, Jean 118
  'Joan with a hat' *75*
Basil, André 119
Beaton, Cecil 18, 20, 48, *48*, 49
  *Fashion: An Anthology by Cecil
  Beaton* 10, 10-11, *20*, *20*, 47,
  49
  The Glass of Fashion 48, 75
  My Fair Lady costumes *20*,
  23, 32, 48, 49, *49*
Ben Yusuf, Anna 118
Ben Yusuf, Zaida 118
berets *12*, 13, 18, *18*, 25, 36, *36*,
  108, *109*
  rubber *73*
Bergdorf Goodman
  department store, New York
  90, 11, 9, 121
Bernstock, Paul *see* Bernstock
  Speirs
Bernstock Speirs 10, 118
Bertin, Rose 15, 16, 77, 118
Bes Ben 31, 69, 118
Beyoncé *73*
Biba 88, *88*, 93
Bierendonck, Walter van 55
Björk *103*, 118
Blaize, Immodesty *38*, 39
Blass, Bill 119, 122
Blige, Mary J. 99
Blitz club, London 18, 20
Blow, Isabella 96, *97*, 121
Bouché, René: illustrations
  25, *82*
Bowen, Kim *19*, 20
Boy George 20, *20*
Boyd, John 118
  felt hat 108
'Breeze Hat Grip' 106, *106*
Bricard, Mitza (Germaine)
  111, 119
  silk headscarf *110*
British Home Stores (BHS) 121
Brooke Davis, Carolyn *see*
  Bare, Fred
Buckley, Jo 88
buckram 61
Bush, Laura 119
Byers, Margaretta: *Designing
  Women* 106

CA4LA 80
Campbell, Ethyle 10
Cardin, Pierre 120
Carmen Miranda 119
Cartland, Dame Barbara *102*
Cavanagh 20
Chanel, Gabrielle (Coco)/
  House of Chanel 16, 28, 6,
  6, *66*, 119, 120, 121, 122
Cholmondeley, Sybil,
  Marchioness of *41*
Churchill, Clementine 93, *93*
cloches, 1920s *9*, 105

'Coconut Willy' 69
Colby, Anita 90
Comme des Garçons 22, *22*,
  112, *112*
Cooper, Lady Diana 99, *99*
Coptic fez hat *25*, 39
Costelloe, Paul 121
Craig, William Marshall:
  Buy a Bonnet Box 74
Crawford, Joan 118
Creed, Charles 122
Crown, Peter Lewis 17
Cullen, Oriole 22, 23

Daché, Lilly 31, *68*, 69, 119, 121
  millinery salon 87, *87*
Day, Robin 18
Death in Venice (film) 119
Debenhams department store
  121, 122
Degas, Edgar 80
  At the Millinery Shop 81
Deneuve, Catherine 118
Denford, Carol and Nigel: 'The
  Hat Shop' 88, 119
Dessès 20
Diana, Princess 108, *109*,
  118, 121
Dietrich, Marlene *12*, 13
Dior, Christian *6*, 16, 20, 22, *52*,
  55, *62*, 112, 11, 5, 120
  hats by Bricard *110*, 111, 119
  hats by Jones 23, *24*, 62, *62*,
  63, *101*, *114*, 115, *117*
Dolores 57, 70
Dr T and the Women (film) 119
Duff Gordon, Lady Lucy *see*
  Lucile
du Mortier, Bianca M.:
  Chapeau, Chapeaux! 83
Dunand, Jean 31, 87, *87*
Dunaway, Faye 108, *109*

Ehrlich, Lola *see* Lola
Elizabeth, the Queen Mother
  20, 95, 120, 121
Elizabeth II 43, 108, *108*, 119,
  120, 121
Elliott, Missy 99, *101*
Esling, Philippa 10, *11*
Eugénie, Empress 25, 120
Evagora, Anita *see* Bare, Fred

Face, The (magazine) 73
Fath, Jacques 16, 22
feather hats *14*, 15, 22, *22*, 27,
  36, 39, *41*, 71, 9, 6, *97*
felt hats *11*, 15, 59, *59*, 61, 108
Firbank, Heather 66
Flora, House of (Flora
  McLean) 119
  rubber beret *73*
flying hat 106, *107*
Fontaine, Joan *43*
Fonteyn, Dame Margot 23,
  93, 122
Ford, Tom 120
Forester, Mrs C. W. 84
Fox, Frederick 57, 71, *102*, 119
  'Coniston' hat 43, *44*
Frowick, Roy Halston *see*
  Halston
fur hats *25*, 59, *103*

Galliano, John *6*, 7, 14, 18,
  25, 112
  hats by Jones *14*, *29*, *46*, *54*,
  55, *63*, *113*
Gap, The 120
Garbo, Greta 118
Garland, Madge 69
Gaultier, Jean Paul *39*, 112
Georgette, Mme 119
Giles 22
Ginsburg, Madeleine 20
Givenchy 99, 112
Goalen, Barbara 18, *18*
Gone With the Wind (film) 119
Gordon, Jane 91
Gordon, Jo 119
Gottschalk, June Gordon *44*
*Grandes Modes de Paris Revue...,
  Les 8*
Greenburg, Adrian *see* Adrian,
  Gilbert

Green Field, Benjamin B. *see*
  Bes Ben
Griffe, Jacques 121
Gucci 120
Guevara, 'Che' 108, *108*

Halston (Roy Halston Frowick)
  16, *90*, 99, 119
Harada, Misa 88, 119
Harburger (Harberger), John
  see John Frederics
Harrods, London 66, *84*, 121
Hartnell, Norman 18, 111, 120
  coat *111*
Hat Magazine, The 119
hatboxes *74*, 74-5, *75*
Haynes, Michael 20, 49
Heath, Henry 106
Heath, Lady Mary 106, 119
Heim, Jacques 121
Hepburn, Audrey 23, 49, *49*
Hex, Shirley 17, 18, 62, *70*, 71,
  71, 119, 121
Hirst, Frederic *see* John
  Frederics
Hochsmann, Gertrud 120
Holmfeld, Lipp 121
Hudson, Kate 119
Hulanicki, Barbara 93
Hyper Hyper, London (store)
  122

Jackson, Michael 118
Jacobs, Marc 22, 55, 112, 122
James, Charles: jacket 17, *17*
Jeans, Earl 120
John Frederics 69, 87, 118, 119
Johnson, Herbert 120
Jones, Grace 118, 119
Jones, Stephen *6*, 7, 9, 10, 11,
  11, 13-25, *27*, *32*, 39, *39*, 49,
  51, *70*, 77, 95
  Anubis head mask *114*, 115
  'Arrow' hat 23, *24*
  ballet shoes hat *25*
  black knitted hat *13*
  blanket hat *54*, 55
  'Bryce' hat *32*, *33*
  'Carnival' tricorne *38*, 39
  'Catherinette' hats 62, *62*, *63*
  Chapeau Boo-tique
  (exhibition) *89*
  'Costermonger' hat 32, *35*
  crown *22*
  'Desert Rose' collection 32,
  32
  'Fish Bone' hat *14*
  flower hat *117*
  'Folly' hat *34*
  'Gerlinde' hat *20*
  'HQ' hat *78*
  kon tiki hat *30*
  millinery ephemera *34*
  'Orchid' hat *46*
  Princess Diana's hat *108*
  PVC cloche *39*, *41*
  'RHS' hat *34*
  'Roxette' plastic wig hat 105,
  105
  'Sea Anenome' hat 36
  'Shirley in Palm Springs'
  hat *71*
  'Still life' hat *47*
  straw and velvet hat *113*
  'Thunderbird' hat *29*
  'Tube' hat *32*, *34*
  Union Jack top *96*
  'Wash and Go' hat *23*
  see also Stephen Jones
  Millinery
Jonesboy (diffusion line) 56
Josephine, Empress 120
Julia, Princess 20

Kangol 121
Karan, Donna 120
Kawakubo, Rei 22, 95, 112
Kelly, Grace 118
Kennedy, Jacqueline *98*, 99, 119
Keys, Alicia 119
Kinoshita, Mitsumi *53*
Kokin 119
Kors, Michael 120

labels, hat *56*

Lachasse 17, 18, *70*, 62, 71
  see also Michael of Lachasse
Lagerfeld, Karl 118, 121, 122
Lambert, Verne 20
Lang, Fritz: *Metropolis 42*
Lanvin, Jeanne/House of
  Lanvin 16, 66, 118, 119-20
Lanvin Castillo 121
La Renta, Oscar de 119, 122
Lauren, Ralph 120, 121, 122
Lelong, Lucien 93
Lepape, Georges: turban *92*
LeRoy, Louis Hippolyte 120
Liberty's 69, 122
List, Adele 120
Logan, Andrew 20
Lola (Lola Ehrlich) 120
Loren, Sophia 118
Lorenz, Mitzi 119
Lucas, Otto 119
Lucile (Lady Lucy Duff
  Gordon) 16, 66, 77, 120
  bird of paradise feather hat
  39, *41*
  fur and silk ribbon hat *25*
  straw hat *67*

McDonald, Julien 120
McDowell, Colin: *Hats: Status,
  Style and Glamour* 14
Macke, Auguste: *Hatshop 79*
McLean, Flora 71, *see also*
  House of Flora
Macy's department store,
  New York 69
Madonna 95, 99
Malyard (George Mallard) 120
  leather hood 39, *40*
Margaret, Princess 120, 121
Marie Antoinette, Queen
  15, 118
Marie Mercie 120
Marshall, Francis: illustrations
  85, *111*
Mattli, Giuseppe 122
Mazhar, Nasir 72
  'Cube' hat 72
Mendes, Valerie 20
Menkes, Suzy 71
Mercie, Marie *see* Marie Mercie
  mercury, use of 59, 61, *61*
Merry Widow, The 120
Metropolis poster 42
Metternich, Princess 120
Michael of Carlos Place 121
Michael of Lachasse: 'Martian's
  Claw' 43, *45*
Miller, Deborah 57, *57*, 62,
  70, 71
  millinery, early 65-6, 69, 84
Minogue, Kylie 22
Mirman, Simone 120
  'Langoustine Fantasia' hat
  36, *37*
'Miss Jones' (diffusion line) 56
'Mister Smith' *see* Smith,
  Justin
Mobutu, Sese Seko 108
Montana, Claude 112
Moodie, Neil 119
Morgan, Rachel Trevor 88
Morton, Digby 122
  motoring hats, lady's 106
Mouret, Roland 121
Mr Fred 119
Mr John 14, *15*, 16, 69, 118, 119
  millinery salon *86*, 87
Mugler, Thierry 112, 120
Muir, Jean 121
Museum of London 71, *71*
My Fair Lady (film) *20*, 23, 32,
  48, 49, 49, 119
Mynott, Lawrence 20

Nakazawa, Sawa 22
New Romantics 18, 93
New York Times 31, 65, 84
Nike 120
Norell 20
Norman, Thomas 74
Normoyle, J. L. 119

O'Neill, Hugh (department
  store) 83
Ozbek, Rifat *25*, 121

Panizon, Madeleine 111, 120

Paterson, Ronald 122
Paule, Madame 111
Paulette, Madame/Paulette 93,
  120, 121
  turban 39, *39*
Peto, Anthony 120
Piaggi, Anna 13, 27, 96, *96*
Piguet, Robert 120
Poiret, Paul 120
  turbans 92, *92*, 111
Prada turban 93, *93*
Prudence 72, 120
Pugh, Gareth 77
  'Cube' hat (Mazhar) 72
  punk 13, 18, *18*

Reagan, Nancy 118
Rebaté, Lucienne 120
Reboux, Caroline 69, 118, 119,
  120, 122
Rees, Dai 120, 121
Renoir, Pierre Auguste 80
Reslaw Hats 120-21
Rhodes, Zandra 121
Rhys, Jean: *Good Morning,
  Midnight* 91
Ritchie, Mrs 75
Roberts, Julia 119
Robeson, Lesley 22, 55
Rotten, Johnny 18, *18*, 108
Royal College of Art, London
  (RCA) 69, 71, 72
Rudolf 121
  hatboxes *74*, *74*, 75
Russell, Rosalind *43*

St Cyr, Claude (Simone
  Nuadet) 16, 111, 121
  hat *111*
Saint Laurent, Yves 20, 93, 120
St Martin's School of Art
  (Central Saint Martins) 17,
  18, *19*, 28, 62
Sant' Angelo, Giorgio 119
Sardiña, Adolfo *see* Adolfo
Schiaparelli, Elsa 20, 120, 121
  'Shoe Hat' 28, *28*
Scott, L'Wren 25
Sem (Georges Goursat):
  cartoon 66
'Serge' (Sergiu Victor) 122
shellac 59
Shilling, David 96, 99, 121
Shilling, Gertrude 13, *13*, 96,
  98, 99, 121
Signac, Paul 80
  Two Milliners 64
Smith, Graham 121
  Pirelli skull cap 43, *44*
Smith, Justin 72, 121
  pigskin top hat 72
Somerville, Philip 121
Spade, Kate 120
Spandau Ballet 20
  spartre 61
Spears, Britney 119
Speirs, Thelma *see* Bernstock
  Speirs
Stael von Holstein, Baroness
  122
Stephen Jones Millinery 51,
  52, *52*, 53, 55-7, *56-8*, 59, 78,
  78, 80, 91
Stewart, Noel 22, 71, 121
Stone, Sharon 119
Strange, Steve 18, 20
straw hats 36, *36*, 59, 61, *67*,
  83, *113*
  collapsible *60*
  flying hat 106, *107*
Stuart, Jill 122
Suzy, Madame 82, 121
  straw hat *83*
Svend 22, 121

Talbot, Suzanne 31, 69, 119,
  121, 122
Taste of Honey, A (film) 75
Thaarup, Aage 31, 69, 69, *74*,
  91, 118, 121
  Elizabeth II's hat *108*
Thyssen, Chessie von 20

Tissières, Véronique *57*
Tissot, James 80
Tonks, Henry 80
Topham, Marianne: *Philip
  Treacy's Belgravia Hat
  Shop 80-1*
trade schools 65, 66
Treacy, Philip 70, 71, 72, 96, 121
  Belgravia Hat Shop 80, *80-1*
  David Beckham hat *31*
  feather hats 22, *22*, 71, 96, *97*
  pampas grass rasta hat *25*
Trigère, Pauline 119
  turbans 14, *92*, 92-3, *93*
Turlington, Christy *113*
Tyler, Liv 119

Underwood, Patricia 121-2
Ungaro 118

Valentino 121
Valois, Rose 120, 122
Vernier, Madame Rose 122
Victor, Sally 69, 122
  collapsible straw hat *60*
Vogue 82, 111
Von Teese, Dita 14, *100*
Vreeland, Diana 20

Walser (Paul) Ltd *see* Reslaw
  Hats
Wedge, James 69, 122
  felt hat with black
  fringing 69
West, Craig 56
Westwood, Vivienne 72, 120
  Harris Tweed crown 108, *108*
wigs, coloured *104*, 105
Windsor, Duchess of (Wallis
  Simpson) 118, 120
Women, The (film) 43
Women's Institute 84
  armchair hat 28
Woolland Bros 122
Wortley Montague, Lady
  Mary 92

Yamamoto, Yohji 20, *21*